THE TRIAL OF
HENRY KISSINGER

ALSO BY CHRISTOPHER HITCHENS

THE TRIAL OF HENRY KISSINGER

CHRISTOPHER HITCHENS

VERSO

London • New York

First published by Verso 2001
© Christopher Hitchens 2001
Paperback edition first published 2002
© Christopher Hitchens 2002
All rights reserved

1 3 5 7 9 10 8 6 4 2

Verso
UK: 6 Meard Street, London W1F 0EG
USA: 180 Varick Street, New York, NY 10014–4606

Verso is the imprint of New Left Books
www.versobooks.com

ISBN 1–85984–398–0

British Library Cataloguing in Publication Data
A catalogue record for this book is available from the British Library

Library of Congress Cataloging-in-Publication Data
A catalog record for this book is available from the Library of Congress

Typeset by M Rules
Printed in the UK by Biddles Ltd, Guildford and Kings Lynn
Printed in the USA by R. R. Donnelley & Sons

For the brave victims of Henry Kissinger, whose example will easily outlive him, and his "reputation."
And for Joseph Heller, who saw it early and saw it whole:

In Gold's conservative opinion, Kissinger would not be recalled in history as a Bismarck, Metternich or Castlereagh but as an odious schlump who made war gladly. (*Good as Gold*, 1976)

CONTENTS

PREFACE TO THE PAPERBACK EDITION

WHEN THIS LITTLE book first appeared, in what may now seem the prehistoric spring of 2001, it attracted a certain amount of derision in some quarters, and on two grounds. A number of reviewers flatly declined to believe that the evidence presented against Henry Kissinger could be true. Others, willing to credit at least the veracity of the official documents, nonetheless scoffed at the mere idea of bringing such a mighty figure within the orbit of the law.

It says nothing for the author, but a great deal about the subject, to be able to report that the lapse of just one year has brought important and incriminating new disclosures and seen significant new developments. To begin with the disclosures, then, one might instance fresh and conclusive evidence under four of the headings originally discussed here: Indochina, Latin America, East Timor and Washington, DC. And, to follow on with the legal developments, one can now cite important proceedings brought against Kissinger in four democratic countries, including his own. I hope I will not seem to boast if I say that most of these disclosures and initiatives were foreshadowed in the first version of this book. At any rate, they now appear below and any reader may judge by comparison with the unaltered original text.

Indochina

Further material has come to light about both the origins and the conclusion of this terrible episode in American and Asian history. The publication of Larry Berman's *No Peace, No Honor: Nixon, Kissinger and Betrayal in Vietnam* in early 2001 provided further evidence of the secret and illegal diplomacy conducted by Nixon and his associates in the fall of 1968, and discussed on pages 6–18 here as well as in my appendix on page 132. Indeed, it can now be safely said that the record of this disgusting scandal has become, so to speak, a part of the official and recognized record, rather as President Johnson's original provocation in the Gulf of Tonkin is now generally called by its right name. (In his edition of President Johnson's private papers and conversations in the fall of 2001, Professor Michael Beschloss produced first-hand and direct proof that Johnson himself knew at the time that he was lying to the Congress and the world about the episode.)

As for the expiring moments of that hideous war, the month of May 2001 saw the publication of an extraordinary book, *The Last Battle: The Mayaguez Incident and the End of the Vietnam War*. Written by Ralph Wetterhahn, a Vietnam veteran who had decided to stay with the subject, the book establishes beyond doubt by the use of contemporary documents and later interviews that:

a) The crew of the *Mayaguez* were never held on Koh Tang island, the island that was invaded by the United States Marine Corps.

b) The Cambodians had announced that they intended to return the vessel, and had indeed done so even as the bombardment of Cambodian territory was continuing. During that time, the crew was being held on quite another island, named Rong Sam Lem. The statements of Ford and Kissinger, claiming credit for the eventual release and attributing it to the intervention on the wrong island, were knowingly false.

c) American casualties were larger than has ever been admitted: twenty-three men were pointlessly sacrificed in a helicopter crash in Thailand that was never acknowledged as part of the operation. Thus, a total of sixty-four servicemen were sacrificed to "free" forty sailors who had already been let go, and who were not and had never been at the advertised location.

d) As a result of the official panic and confusion, three Marines were left behind alive on Koh Tang island, and later captured and murdered by the Khmer Rouge. The names of Lance Corporal Joseph Hargrove, Pfc Gary Hall and Pvt Danny Marshall do not appear on any memorial, let alone the Vietnam Veterans' wall (see my page 24). For a long time, their names had no official existence at all, and this "denial" might have succeeded indefinitely were it not for Mr Wetterhahn's efforts.

Kissinger was the crucial figure at all stages of this crime and cover-up, arguing at the onset of the crisis that B-52 bombers should at once (and again) be launched against Cambodia and arguing, too, for the dropping of the BLU-82 bomb – a 15,000-pound device – on the center of Koh Tang island. He must also have been crucial in the following hair-raising episode, made public by William Triplett in the official publication of the Vietnam Veterans of America. Mr Triplett interviewed then-Secretary of Defense James Schlesinger, who recalled two cabinet meetings during the crisis. The first was the one at which Kissinger demanded the use of B-52s. The second was the one – no less alarming to Secretary Schlesinger – at which it was decided to sink *all ships* spotted in the vicinity of Koh Tang island. As Schlesinger recalled it:

> When I got [back] to the Pentagon . . . I said that before any ships are sunk, our pilots should fly low over the ships and see what they could see, particularly if there were any [*Mayaguez*] crew members aboard. If they did see them, they were to report back immediately before doing anything. In the course of flying over the area, one of our Navy pilots called back saying that he saw "Caucasians" aboard a ship. . . . Or he thought he saw that. It later turned out that every member of the *Mayaguez* crew was on that ship.

Q: Did you apprise the White House of this ship with the Caucasians aboard?

A: Yes, indeed.

Q: And it was then that the White House said to sink it?

A: Yes, the White House said, "We told you to sink all ships, so sink it!"

By stalling for three hours, the Secretary of Defense managed to avoid committing this atrocity. And by "the White House" he clearly does not mean the President, or he would have said so. In any case, we know who was managing the *Mayaguez* "rescue," and who took credit for it at the time. We are sure to learn even more about Kissinger's "hands-on" policy in Indochina as still more officials write their memoirs or make their confessions.

Latin America

The documentary record on Chile is now more or less complete, but much remains to be discovered about Kissinger's role in Operation Condor (see my pages 67–8), and in the nexus of dictatorship and repression which gave it birth. Recent published work by Martin Edwin Andersen and John Dinges, in the conservative Washington magazine *Insight* in January 2002, has presented us with incontrovertible proof of high-level approval for Argentina's "dirty war" of death and "disappearance" in the mid-1970s.

The evidence here might be described as unimpeachable, since it originates with a senior member of the Argentine dictatorship and an ultra-conservative United States diplomat. The first man, Admiral Cesar Guzzetti, foreign minister of the Videla dictatorship, had a dispute about both means and ends with the second man, US Ambassador Robert Hill. Ambassador Hill was a Cold-War veteran with tight family connections to the business oligarchy in Latin America. A Nixon appointee to the Buenos Aires post, he had also served contentedly as envoy to a number of despotic right-wing regimes. However, he was appalled by the campaign of murder unleashed in Argentina after the 1976 military coup, and became distressed by the way in which Kissinger, from Washington, undercut his representations on the matter.

To those familiar with the Chile investigation, in which a "two-track" policy was pursued and the officially accredited ambassador is not *supposed* to know of the real or covert policy, this may seem unsurprising. But not to Hill, an old-school type, the declassification of whose cables furnishes much of the new material. Before Admiral Guzzetti traveled to Washington to see Kissinger in October 1976, Hill had met him and told him that "murdering priests and dumping forty-seven bodies in the street in one day could not be seen in the context of defeating the terrorists quickly; on the contrary such acts were probably counterproductive. What the USG [United States Government] hoped was that the GOA [Government of Argentina] could soon defeat terrorists, yes, but as nearly as possible within the law."

Even this admonition, which might be seen by some as containing a loophole or two, was considered too harsh by Kissinger. Guzzetti set off for Washington, Hill subsequently minuted, "fully expecting to hear some strong, firm, direct warnings on his government's human rights practices." However, having met Guzzetti on his return to Buenos Aires, he concluded:

> Rather than that, he [Guzzetti] has returned in a state of jubilation, convinced that there is no real problem with the United States over this issue. Based on what Guzzetti is doubtless reporting to the GOA, it must now believe that if it has any problems with the US over human rights, they are confined to certain elements of Congress and what it regards as biased and/or uninformed minor segments of public opinion. . . . While this conviction exists, it will be unrealistic and ineffective for this Embassy to press representations to the GOA over human rights violations.

This is even more grave in its implications than may at first appear. In October 1976 the rate of state-sponsored kidnapping and "disappearance" was relatively slow and could, Ambassador Hill believed, be made slower still. But the declassified documents show Kissinger advising Guzzetti, in effect, to speed up the pace. He told him that "if the terrorist problem was over by December or January, he [Kissinger] believed that serious problems could be avoided in the United States." These and other reassurances were, according to Hill – and in a phrase that has since become obscenely familiar – "the green light" for intensified repression. When Kissinger and Guzzetti first met, the number of "disappeared" was estimated at 1,022. By the time that Argentina had become an international byword for torture, for anti-Semitism, for death-squads and for the concept of the *desaparecido*, a minimum of 15,000 victims had been registered by reliable international and local monitors. In 1978, when the situation was notorious, Kissinger (by then out of office) accepted a personal invitation from the dictator General Videla to be his guest during Argentina's hosting of the soccer World Cup. The former Secretary of State made use of the occasion to lecture the Carter administration for its excessive tenderness concerning human rights. General Videla, with whom I had a horrifying interview at about this time in the Casa Rosada in Buenos Aires, has since been imprisoned for life. One of the more specific charges on which he was convicted was the sale of the children of rape victims held in his secret jails. His patron and protector, meanwhile, is enjoying a patriarchal autumn that may still (see below) be disturbed by the memory of what he permitted and indeed encouraged.

East Timor

On more than one occasion (see my pages 90–107) Henry Kissinger has absolutely and publicly denied that he had any foreknowledge of the Indonesian invasion of East Timor, any interest in the subject, or even any awareness of its importance. That this is a huge falsehood, or perhaps a series of interlocking falsehoods, has long been apparent from independent evidence. What might be called conclusive or "smoking gun" proof, however, only became available in December 2001, when a fresh document became available. Declassified by the State Department, and publicised by the National Security Archive, it is the official record of a conversation that took place in the Indonesian capital of Jakarta on 6 December 1975. Present were Henry Kissinger and Gerald Ford, and the Indonesian dictator Suharto with a group of his military advisors.

Since Kissinger himself had received a cable from Washington two days before, informing him that the Indonesian junta had "plans" to invade East Timor, he cannot have been very much surprised to be told exactly that. Nor can he have been startled to hear from Suharto that: "We want your understanding if we deem it necessary to take rapid or drastic action." President Ford did not attempt to mask his endorsement in any ambiguity. "We will understand and will not press you on the issue," he said. "We understand the problem and the intentions you have." Kissinger, more experienced in the spin-problems that could result from unleashing extremist dictatorships, employed language similar to that which he had (see above) lavished upon Admiral Guzzetti of Argentina. "The use of US-made arms could create problems," he mused, adding that "it depends on how we construe it; whether it is in self-defense or a foreign operation." This was an absolute untruth, since (see my page 103) Kissinger knew perfectly well that the use of American-*supplied* (not "American made") weaponry would violate international law and United States law as well. Brightening somewhat, he assured Suharto that: "We would be able to influence the reaction in America if whatever happens happens after we return . . . If you have made plans, we will do our best to keep everyone quiet until the President returns home." As ever, he was willing to act as errand-boy for an unelected foreign dictatorship and to consider only Congress as his enemy.

It was therefore agreed, in an early instance of the now-famous pseudo-science of "deniability," that the aggression be timed to suit the fact that "The President will be back on Monday at 2.00 pm Jakarta time. We understand your problem and the need to move quickly but I am only saying that it would be better if it were done after we returned." With these words, Kissinger made himself directly complicit in the letter and the spirit of Indonesia's attack. A certain nervousness prompted him to ask Suharto if he anticipated "a long guerrilla war"; proof in itself that he did not believe Suharto's claim of popular support in East Timor. The dictator was reassuring, predicting that there would "probably be a short guerrilla war," while refusing to be drawn on its actual duration. The announced imperative of speed, as in Argentina above, was a spur to ruthless methods that had in effect been demanded by Washington. "It is important," said Kissinger coldly, "that whatever you do succeeds quickly." The consequences of this deadly injunction are discussed on my pages 91–2.

The same memorandum shows that the talk then turned to Indonesia's oil policy, and to Suharto's complaint that major petroleum corporations shared more of the wealth with their Middle Eastern partners than they did with Indonesia. Expressing sympathy for his attempt to negotiate a better deal, Kissinger found time to warn the despot that, whatever he did, he should "not create a climate that discourages investment." This was a case of pushing at an open door: to the very end of his regime Suharto maintained an investment-friendly climate, at least for a certain class of cronies of whom, perhaps coincidentally (see my pages 124–6), Kissinger eventually became one. Indeed, Indonesian "crony capitalism" and its practitioners became a major element in the scandal of United States campaign finance, and of the Congressional investigation into it, that marked the Clinton years. Kissinger even hired Clinton's former White House Chief of Staff Mack McLarty as a partner in Kissinger Associates, and it may not be fanciful to suppose that the Indonesian connection played a role in this beautiful piece of bipartisanship.

The Suharto regime collapsed and imploded between the years 2000 and 2001. East Timor won its independence, and Indonesia formally withdrew its claim to the territory. Suharto himself was indicted by the Indonesian courts for corruption and only escaped the verdict by resorting, as had General Pinochet, to the claim of mental and physical incompetence. Once again, though, the senior partner in the massacres and in the corruption managed to escape condemnation.

Washington

As I was preparing to publish the original version of this book, I received a call from William Rogers. Mr Rogers is a partner in the distinguished Washington law firm of Arnold and Porter and was, during Kissinger's period as Secretary of State, the Deputy Assistant Secretary for Inter-American Affairs. He is also a cog in the wheel of Kissinger Associates (for the activities of which, see chapter 10). Someone had leaked the advance news of publication to a New York newspaper and Mr Rogers, on first contact, was all friendliness. Could he help? he wanted to know. I told him that I had already forwarded a request for an interview to his boss, and had mentioned the headings – Chile, Timor, Bangladesh and the Demetracopoulos affair – which I hoped to discuss with him. Mr Rogers professed astonishment at the fourth of these topics. "Who is this guy Demetra-whatsisname?" he inquired. "We've never heard of him." He then asked me to send a list of all my questions, in order that he might be more "helpful" still. Recognising a fishing expedition when I saw one, I instead wrote again to Kissinger offering to pay him for his trouble and proposing that, if he would give me and *Harper's* magazine half an hour on the record, we would pay him at the same rate offered by ABC News *Nightline*. (I did not add that, for this honorarium, we would ask him all the questions he has never been asked by Mr Ted Koppel.)

Mr Rogers then dropped the mask of pretended if inquisitive politeness and sent me a savage e-mail, in which he said that he had never heard of such a disgraceful proposal. How could I, he demanded to know, propose to pay a source? Quite obviously I was morally unfit for further conversation. His indignation got the better of him. I was only making an ironic reference to Kissinger's habit of charging immense fees for his time (and at no period did I think of him as a "source"). I wrote back to Rogers, saying that he seemed to be the same man who had attended the Kissinger–Pinochet private discussion on 8 June 1976 (see my pages 69–71) during which Pinochet had threatened a Chilean exile then living in Washington. On that occasion, I pointed out, the record showed that Mr

Rogers had sat in silence. It was therefore good to know what did, and what did not, touch his nerve of outrage. Mr Rogers, it now turns out, also played a role in facilitating the Kissinger–Guzzetti conversations in 1976, and later in trying to put a positive shine upon them. Such men are always, it seems, with us.

The absurdity of the official pretense, that Elias Demetracopoulos was beneath Kissinger's notice, is even further exposed by a recently declassified letter from Kissinger to Nixon, sent on 22 March 1971. It is headed "SECRET: The Demetracopoulos Affair." It begins by saying to the President: "You may have heard some repercussions from the recent flap over a request by Greek 'journalist' and resistance leader, Elias Demetracopoulos, to return to Greece to see his sick father." (It's rather flattering that Kissinger should have put "journalist" in sarcastic quotes, but left the definition of resistance leader unamended.) The letter goes on to say:

> Since Demetracopoulos has such a following in Congress and has an outlet in Rowland Evans [then a senior Washington columnist] I thought you might be interested in knowing that he has long been an irritant in US–Greek relations. Among his intrigues – which have included selling himself as a trusted US agent to anyone and everyone – he has touched off a record number of controversies and embarrassments between Greek and American officials. Through various journalistic enterprises, he has somehow managed to gain access to press and government circles. CIA, State, Defense and USIA have repeatedly warned officials about Demetracopoulos . . .

It would appear safe to say, then, that Demetracopoulos was taken with sufficient seriousness by Kissinger to warrant a slanderous and paranoid memorandum for the President's desk. This only strengthens the argument made in my chapter 9, that Kissinger was attempting to represent his Greek critic as a person dangerous and sinister enough to be dealt with.

Another declassified secret document, this time of a "Secretary's

Analytical Staff Meeting" at the State Department on 20 March 1974, shows Kissinger's obsession at work again. Irritated by talk of a return to constitutional rule in Greece, he said: "My question is: Why is it in the American interest to do in Greece what we apparently don't do anywhere else – of requiring them to give a commitment to the President to move to representative government?"

This was only a few months after the existing right-wing dictatorship in Athens had been overthrown from the extreme right by the psychopath Brigadier Ioannidis. Even Henry Tasca, then United States Ambassador to Athens and a trusted friend of the regime, was moved to reply:

> Well, I think because Greece and the Greek people – in terms of their position and public opinion in Western Europe – are quite unique. You can go back to the constitutional Greece or the Greek lobby – whatever you want to call it – and they've got a position in Western Europe and the United States that Brazil and Chile and these other countries don't have. None of these countries has a Demetracopoulos – a Greek refugee who's been activated and who for four years has been leading a very vigorous fight on our policy in Greece.

To this Kissinger made the glacial reply that "That just means we're letting Demetracopoulos's particular group make policy." But he was clearly nettled that some of his own deputies found it difficult to treat Greece as a banana republic.

This was a high-level meeting. The minutes record the attendance of such policy heavyweights as Joseph Sisco, Helmut Sonnenfeld, Lawrence Eagleburger and Arthur Hartman. It is clear that the dangerous activity of a single dissident was not beneath official attention.

Once again, I note that the Greek government, for which Kissinger was acting as proxy here, was a murderous and torturing dictatorship, with aggressive designs upon its Cypriot neighbor, and that its then-leaders are now in prison for life. And once again, I note that their senior partner and patron is still at liberty, and still lying about his part in all this.

LEGAL CONSEQUENCES

Just as this book was being published, Kissinger produced a volume of his own with the pseudo-solemn title *Does America Need a Foreign Policy?* It contained an anxious chapter on the perils of the new legal doctrine of "universal jurisdiction," and this same chapter was reprinted as a separate essay in the Establishment's house-organ *Foreign Affairs.* There was a certain amount of public laughter at the sheer disingenuousness of this: Kissinger wrote as if he was cogitating the subject with absolute disinterest.

Events, however, were to give independent validation of his professed concern. In May 2001, Judge Rodolfo Corral, a senior magistrate in Argentina, issued a summons to Kissinger to answer questions about his knowledge of Operation Condor (see my pages 67–8). Judge Corral's investigation, like many similar human rights inquiries in the southern hemisphere of the Americas, could proceed no further without disclosure of what the United States knew and when it knew it, and Kissinger was the chief material witness at all material times.

Only a few days later, on 28 May 2001, Kissinger was visited in his suite at the Ritz Hotel in Paris by the criminal division of the French *gendarmerie.* They brought him a summons, issued by Judge Roger Le Loire, to appear at the Palais de Justice the following morning and answer questions about the "disappearance" of five French citizens in Chile during the early days of the Pinochet regime. Kissinger might reasonably have thought himself safe in the hotel owned by Mohammed al-Fayed, but chose the path of prudence and left Paris at once. (The summons remains valid if he should ever choose to return; I should like to boast briefly that the European press attributed this judicial move in part to the then-recent appearance of this book in its French translation.)

Since then, the Chilean courts – including the judge who is deciding the Pinochet case itself – have written to Kissinger asking for his cooperation as a witness in the case of Charles Horman, an American reporter murdered during Pinochet's coup, and in the general matter of "Condor"-related crime.

This means that duly constituted magistrates in three democratic nations are seeking – and are being refused – his testimony on grave crimes against humanity. As predicted in my introduction (see pages 1–5) he can no longer make travel plans without consulting his expensive attorneys.

Most serious of all, though, was the suit filed in Federal Court in Washington, DC, on 10 September 2001. This suit is brought by the surviving members of the family of General Rene Schneider of Chile (see my pages 56–66 and 131). It charges Kissinger and others with "summary execution" of the General; in other words, but in a civil case, with murder and international terrorism. The date of the lawsuit may seem unpropitious to some, but in fact the hideous aggression against American civil society that occurred the following day has laid greater emphasis than ever on the need for a single standard, and one day a single international court, for the hearing of crimes against humanity, state-sponsored murder and international nihilism.

In the same period, the National Security Archive and others compelled Kissinger to return 50,000 pages of the public documents he had illegally abstracted when he left office (see my page 76) and to have these returned to the scrutiny of scholars and historians (and victims). It is an empirically safe bet that Kissinger did not seek to conceal or bury material that put him in a good light. We may therefore expect the coming years to be as full of appalling disclosure, of official crime and official lying on his part, as the last year has been. And there is a just a chance that some of the victims may secure some justice on their own account, by means of American and other courts. It seems to me deplorable, though, and even shameful, that those who have already suffered enough should have to volunteer for the performance of a task that properly lies on the shoulders of Congress and the Justice Department.

To leave a personal note to the very last, I had myself rather hoped to be engaged in litigation with Kissinger. Had he sued me over this book (as the London *Literary Review* said that he was in honor bound to do, if he valued his reputation) I had dreamed of producing witnesses, and subpoenaing documents, that would accelerate the process of discovery. It was not to be: Kissinger's reticence remained his best counsel. I did, however, find myself threatening to sue him when he publicly accused me of being an anti-Semite and a denier of the Holocaust. In very grudging and graceless terms, he did through his lawyers offer me a swift retraction. In other words, he admitted that he had no basis for this especially foul accusation, but had thought it worth trying. Those who are curious to learn the background and to follow the correspondence may direct their trusty search-engines and browsers to my site at www.enteract.com/~peterk.

Christopher Hitchens
Washington, DC, 15 February 2002

IT WILL BECOME clear, and may as well be stated at the outset, that this book is written by a political opponent of Henry Kissinger. Nonetheless, I have found myself continually amazed at how much hostile and discreditable material I have felt compelled to omit. I am concerned only with those Kissingerian offenses that might or should form the basis of a legal prosecution: for war crimes, for crimes against humanity, and for offenses against common or customary or international law, including conspiracy to commit murder, kidnap and torture.

Thus, in my capacity as a political opponent I might have mentioned Kissinger's recruitment and betrayal of the Iraqi Kurds, who were falsely encouraged by him to take up arms against Saddam Hussein in 1974–75, and who were then abandoned to extermination on their hillsides when Saddam Hussein made a diplomatic deal with the Shah of Iran, and who were deliberately lied to as well as abandoned. The conclusions of the report by Congressman Otis Pike still make shocking reading, and reveal on Kissinger's part a callous indifference to human life and human rights. But they fall into the category of depraved realpolitik, and do not seem to have violated any known law.

In the same way, Kissinger's orchestration of political and military and diplomatic cover for apartheid in South Africa and the South African destabilization of Angola, with its appalling consequences, presents us with a morally repulsive record. Again, though, one is looking at a sordid period of Cold War and imperial history, and an exercise of irresponsible power, rather than an episode of organized crime. Additionally, one must take into account the institutional nature of this policy, which might in outline have been followed under any administration, national security advisor, or secretary of state.

Similar reservations can be held about Kissinger's chairmanship of the Presidential Commission on Central America in the early 1980s, which was staffed by Oliver North and which whitewashed death squad activity in the isthmus. Or about the political protection provided by Kissinger, while in office, for the Pahlavi dynasty in Iran and its machinery of torture and repression. The list, it is sobering to say, could be protracted very much further. But it will not do to blame the whole exorbitant cruelty and cynicism of decades on one man. (Occasionally one gets an intriguing glimpse, as when Kissinger urges President Ford not to receive the inconvenient Alexander Solzhenitsyn, while all the time he poses as Communism's most daring and principled foe.)

No, I have confined myself to the identifiable crimes that can and should be placed on a proper bill of indictment, whether the actions taken were in line with general "policy" or not. These include:

1. The deliberate mass killing of civilian populations in Indochina.
2. Deliberate collusion in mass murder, and later in assassination, in Bangladesh.
3. The personal suborning and planning of murder, of a senior constitutional officer in a democratic nation – Chile – with which the United States was not at war.
4. Personal involvement in a plan to murder the head of state in the democratic nation of Cyprus.
5. The incitement and enabling of genocide in East Timor.
6. Personal involvement in a plan to kidnap and murder a journalist living in Washington, DC.

The above allegations are not exhaustive. And some of them can only be constructed *prima facie*, since Mr Kissinger – in what may also amount to a deliberate and premeditated obstruction of justice – has caused large tranches of evidence to be withheld or destroyed.

However, we now enter upon the age when the defense of "sovereign immunity" for state crimes has been held to be void. As I demonstrate below, Kissinger has understood this decisive change even if many of his critics have not. The Pinochet verdict in London, the splendid activism of the Spanish magistracy, and the verdicts of the International Tribunal at The Hague have destroyed the shield that immunized crimes committed under the justification of *raison d'état*. There is now no reason why a warrant for the trial of Kissinger may not be issued, in any one of a number of jurisdictions, and why he may not be compelled to answer it. Indeed, and as I write, there are a number of jurisdictions where the law is at long last beginning to catch up with the evidence. And we have before us in any case the Nuremberg precedent, by which the United States solemnly undertook to be bound.

A failure to proceed will constitute a double or triple offense to justice. First, it will violate the essential and now uncontested principle that not even the most powerful are above the law. Second, it will suggest that prosecutions for war crimes and crimes against humanity are reserved for losers, or for minor despots in relatively negligible countries. This in turn will lead to the paltry politicization of what could have been a noble process, and to the justifiable suspicion of double standards.

Many if not most of Kissinger's partners in crime are now in jail, or are awaiting trial, or have been otherwise punished or discredited. His own lonely impunity is rank; it smells to heaven. If it is allowed to persist then we shall shamefully vindicate the ancient philosopher Anacharsis, who maintained that laws were like cobwebs: strong enough to detain only the weak, and too weak to hold the strong. In the name of innumerable victims known and unknown, it is time for justice to take a hand.

INTRODUCTION

ON 2 DECEMBER 1998, Mr Michael Korda was being interviewed on camera in his office at Simon and Schuster. As one of the reigning magnates of New York publishing, he had edited and "produced" the work of authors as various as Tennessee Williams, Richard Nixon, Joan Crawford and Jo Bonanno. On this particular day, he was talking about the life and thoughts of Cher, whose portrait adorned the wall behind him. And then the telephone rang and there was a message to call "Dr" Henry Kissinger as soon as possible. A polymath like Mr Korda knows – what with the exigencies of publishing in these vertiginous days – how to switch in an instant between Cher and high statecraft. The camera kept running, and recorded the following scene for a tape which I possess.

Asking his secretary to get the number (759 7919 – the digits of Kissinger Associates) Mr Korda quips drily, to general laughter in the office, that it "should be 1-800-CAMBODIA . . . 1-800-BOMB-CAMBODIA." After a pause of nicely calibrated duration (no senior editor likes to be put on hold while he's receiving company, especially media company), it's "Henry – Hi, how are you? . . . You're getting all the publicity you could want in the *New York Times*, but not the *kind* you want. . . . I also think it's very, very dubious for the administration to simply say yes, they'll release these papers . . . no . . . no, absolutely . . . no . . . no . . . well, hmmm, yeah. We did it until quite recently, frankly, and he did prevail. . . . Well, I don't think there's any question about that, as uncomfortable as it may be. . . . Henry, this is totally outrageous . . . yeah. . . . Also the jurisdiction. This is a Spanish judge appealing to an English court about a Chilean head of state. So it's, it. . . . Also Spain has no rational jurisdiction over events in Chile anyway so that makes absolutely no sense. . . . Well, that's probably true. . . . If you would. I think that would be by far and away the best. . . . Right, yeah, no I think it's exactly what you should do and I think it should be long and I think it should end with your father's letter. I think it's a very important document. . . . Yes, but I think the letter is wonderful, and central to the entire book. Can you let me read the Lebanon chapter over the weekend?" At this point the conversation ends, with some jocular observations by Mr Korda about his upcoming colonoscopy: "a totally repulsive procedure."

By means of the same tiny internal camera, or its forensic equivalent, one could deduce not a little about the world of Henry Kissinger from this microcosmic exchange. The first and most important thing is this. Sitting in his office at Kissinger Associates, with its tentacles of business and consultancy stretching from Belgrade to Beijing, and cushioned by innumerable other directorships and boards, he still shudders when he hears of the arrest of a dictator. Syncopated the conversation with Mr Korda may be, but it's clear that the keyword is "jurisdiction." What had the *New York Times* been reporting that fine morning? On that 2 December 1998, its front page carried the following report from Tim Weiner, the paper's national security correspondent in Washington. Under the headline "U.S. Will Release Files on Crimes Under Pinochet," he wrote:

> Treading into a political and diplomatic confrontation it tried to avoid, the United States decided today to declassify some secret documents on the killings and torture committed during the dictatorship of Augusto Pinochet in Chile. . . . The decision to release such documents is the first sign that the United States will cooperate in the case against General Pinochet. Clinton Administration officials said they believed the benefits of openness in human rights cases outweighed the risks to national security in this case.

But the decision could open "a can of worms," in the words of a former Central Intelligence Agency official stationed in Chile, exposing the depth of the knowledge that the United States had about crimes charged against the Pinochet Government ...

While some European government officials have supported bringing the former dictator to court, United States officials have stayed largely silent, reflecting skepticism about the Spanish court's power, doubts about international tribunals aimed at former foreign rulers, *and worries over the implications for American leaders who might someday also be accused in foreign countries.* [italics added]

President Richard M. Nixon and Henry A. Kissinger, who served as his national security advisor and Secretary of State, supported a right-wing coup in Chile in the early 1970s, previously declassified documents show.

But many of the actions of the United States during the 1973 coup, and much of what American leaders and intelligence services did in liaison with the Pinochet government after it seized power, remain under the seal of national security. The secret files on the Pinochet regime are held by the CIA, the Defense Intelligence Agency, the State Department, the Pentagon, the National Security Council, the National Archives, the Presidential libraries of Gerald R. Ford and Jimmy Carter, and other Government agencies.

According to Justice Department records, these files contain a history of human rights abuses and international terrorism:

- In 1975 State Department officials in Chile protested the Pinochet regime's record of killing and torture, filing dissents to American foreign policy with their superiors in Washington.
- The CIA has files on assassinations by the regime and the Chilean secret police. The intelligence agency also has records on Chile's attempts to establish an international right-wing covert-action squad.
- The Ford Library contains many of Mr Kissinger's secret files on Chile, which have never been made public. Through a secretary, Mr Kissinger declined a request for an interview today.

One must credit Kissinger with grasping what so many other people did not: that if the Pinochet precedent became established, then he himself was in some danger. The United States believes that it alone pursues and indicts war criminals and "international terrorists"; nothing in its political or journalistic culture yet allows for the thought that it might be harboring and sheltering such a senior one. Yet the thought had very obliquely surfaced in Mr Weiner's story, and Kissinger was a worried man when he called his editor that day to discuss a memoir (eventually published under the unbearably dull and self-regarding title *Years of Renewal*) that was still in progress.

"Harboring and sheltering," though, are understatements for the lavishness of Henry Kissinger's circumstances. His advice is sought, at $25,000 an appearance, by audiences of businessmen and academics and policymakers. His turgid newspaper column is syndicated by the *Los Angeles Times*. His first volume of memoirs was part written and also edited by Harold Evans, who with Tina Brown is among the many hosts and hostesses who solicit Kissinger's company, or perhaps one should say society, for those telling New York soirées. At different times, he has been a consultant to ABC News and CBS; his most successful diplomacy, indeed, has probably been conducted with the media (and his single greatest achievement has been to get almost everybody to call him "Doctor"). Fawned on by Ted Koppel, sought out by corporations and despots with "image" problems or "failures of communication," and given respectful attention by presidential candidates and those whose task it is to "mold" their global vision, this man wants for little in the pathetic universe that the "self-esteem" industry exists to serve. Of whom else would Norman Podhoretz write, in a bended-knee encomium to *Years of Upheaval*:

> What we have here is writing of the very highest order. It is writing that is equally at ease in portraiture and abstract analysis; that can shape a narrative as skillfully as it can paint a scene; that can achieve marvels of compression while moving at an expansive and leisurely pace. It is writing that can shift without strain or falsity of tone from the *gravitas* befitting a book about great historical events to the humor and irony dictated by an unfailing sense of human proportion.

A critic who can suck like that, as was once drily said by one of my moral tutors, need never dine alone. And nor need his subject. Except that, every now and then, the recipient (and donor) of so much sycophancy feels a tremor of anxiety. He leaves the well-furnished table and scurries to the bathroom. Is it perhaps another disclosure on a newly released Nixon tape? Some stray news from Indonesia, portending the fall or imprisonment of another patron (and perhaps the escape of an awkward document or two)? The arrest or indictment of a torturer or assassin, the expiry of the statute of secrecy for some obscure cabinet papers in a faraway country – any one of these can instantly spoil his day. As we see from the Korda tape, Kissinger cannot open the morning paper with the assurance of tranquillity. Because he knows what others can only suspect, or guess at. He knows. And he is a prisoner of the knowledge as, to some extent, are we.

Notice the likeable way in which Mr Korda demonstrates his broad-mindedness with the Cambodia jest. Everybody "knows," after all, that Kissinger inflicted terror and misery and mass death on that country, and great injury to the United States Constitution at the same time. (Everybody also "knows" that other vulnerable nations can lay claim to the same melancholy and hateful distinction, with incremental or "collateral" damage to American democracy keeping pace.) Yet the pudgy man standing in black tie at the *Vogue* party is not, surely, the man who ordered and sanctioned the destruction of civilian populations, the assassination of inconvenient politicians, the kidnapping and disappearance of soldiers and journalists and clerics who got in his way? Oh, but he *is*. It's exactly the same man. And that may be among the most nauseating reflections of all. Kissinger is not invited and feted because of his exquisite manners or his mordant wit (his manners are in any case rather gross, and his wit consists of a quiver of borrowed and secondhand darts). No, he is sought after because his presence supplies a *frisson*: the authentic touch of raw and unapologetic power. There's a slight guilty nervousness on the edge of Mr Korda's gag about the indescribable sufferings of Indochina. And I've noticed, time and again standing at the back of the audience during Kissinger speeches, that laughter of the nervous, uneasy kind is the sort of laughter he likes to provoke. In exacting this tribute, he flaunts not the "aphrodisiac" of power (another of his plagiarized *bons mots*) but its pornography.

1

CURTAIN-RAISER: THE SECRET OF '68

THERE EXISTS, WITHIN the political class of Washington, DC, an open secret that is too momentous and too awful to tell. Though it is well known to academic historians, senior reporters, former cabinet members and ex-diplomats, it has never been summarized all at one time in any one place. The reason for this is, on first viewing, paradoxical. The open secret is in the possession of both major political parties, and it directly implicates the past statecraft of at least three former presidencies. Thus, its full disclosure would be in the interest of no particular faction. Its truth is therefore the guarantee of its obscurity; it lies like Poe's "purloined letter" across the very aisle that signifies bipartisanship.

Here is the secret in plain words. In the fall of 1968, Richard Nixon and some of his emissaries and underlings set out to sabotage the Paris peace negotiations on Vietnam. The means they chose were simple: they privately assured the South Vietnamese military rulers that an incoming Republican regime would offer them a better deal than would a Democratic one. In this way, they undercut both the talks themselves and the electoral strategy of Vice-President Hubert Humphrey. The tactic "worked," in that the South Vietnamese junta withdrew from the talks on the eve of the election, thereby destroying the "peace plank" on which the Democrats had contested it. In another way, it did not "work," because four years later the Nixon administration concluded the war on the same terms that had been on offer in Paris. The reason for the dead silence that still surrounds the question is that, in those intervening four years, some twenty thousand Americans and an uncalculated number of Vietnamese, Cambodians and Laotians lost their lives. Lost them, that is to say, even more pointlessly than had those slain up to that point. The impact of those four years on Indochinese society, and on American democracy, is beyond computation. The chief beneficiary of the covert action, and of the subsequent slaughter, was Henry Kissinger.

I can already hear the guardians of consensus scraping their blunted quills to describe this as a "conspiracy theory." I happily accept the challenge. Let us take, first, the White House journal of that renowned conspirator (and theorist of conspiracy) H.R. Haldeman, published in May 1994. I choose to start with this for two reasons. First, because, on the logical inference of "evidence against interest," it is improbable that Mr Haldeman would supply evidence of his knowledge of a crime unless he was (posthumously) telling the truth. Second, because it is possible to trace back each of his entries to its origin in other documented sources.

In January 1973, the Nixon–Kissinger administration – for which Mr Haldeman took the minutes – was heavily engaged on two fronts. In Paris, Henry Kissinger was striving to negotiate "peace with honor" in Vietnam. In Washington, DC, the web of evidence against the Watergate burglars and buggers was beginning to tighten. On 8 January 1973, Haldeman records:

> John Dean called to report on the Watergate trials, says that if we can prove in any way by hard evidence that our [campaign] plane was bugged in '68, he thinks that we could use that as a basis to say we're going to force Congress to go back and investigate '68 as well as '72, and thus turn them off.

Three days later, on 11 January 1973, Haldeman hears from Nixon ("The P," as the *Diaries* call him):

> On the Watergate question, he wanted me to talk to [Attorney General John] Mitchell and have him find out from [Deke] De Loach [of the FBI] if the guy

who did the bugging on us in 1968 is still at the FBI, and then [FBI acting director Patrick] Gray should nail him with a lie detector and get it settled, which would give us the evidence we need. He also thinks I ought to move with George Christian [President Johnson's former press secretary, then working with Democrats for Nixon], get LBJ to use his influence to turn off the Hill investigation with Califano, Hubert, and so on. Later in the day, he decided that wasn't such a good idea, and told me not to do it, which I fortunately hadn't done.

On the same day, Haldeman reports Henry Kissinger calling excitedly from Paris, saying "he'll do the signing in Paris rather than Hanoi, which is the key thing." He speaks also of getting South Vietnam's President Thieu to "go along." On the following day:

> The P also got back on the Watergate thing today, making the point that I should talk to Connally about the Johnson bugging process to get his judgement as to how to handle it. He wonders if we shouldn't just have Andreas go in and scare Hubert. The problem in going at LBJ is how he'd react, and we need to find out from De Loach who did it, and then run a lie detector on him. I talked to Mitchell on the phone on this subject and he said De Loach had told him he was up to date on the thing because he had a call from Texas. A *Star* reporter was making an inquiry in the last week or so, and LBJ got very hot and called Deke [De Loach] and said to him that if the Nixon people are going to play with this, that he would release [*deleted material – national security*], saying that our side was asking that certain things be done. By our side, I assume he means the Nixon campaign organization. De Loach took this as a direct threat from Johnson. . . . As he recalls it, bugging was requested on the planes, but was turned down, and all they did was check the phone calls, and put a tap on the Dragon Lady [Mrs Anna Chennault].

This bureaucratic prose may be hard to read, but it needs no cypher to decode itself. Under intense pressure about the bugging of the Watergate building, Nixon instructed his chief of staff Haldeman, and his FBI contact Deke De Loach, to unmask the bugging to which his own campaign had been subjected in 1968. He also sounded out former President Johnson, through former senior Democrats like Governor John Connally, to gauge what his reaction to the disclosure might be. The aim was to show that "everybody does it." (By another bipartisan paradox, in Washington the slogan "they all do it" is used as a slogan for the defense rather than, as one might hope, for the prosecution.)

However, a problem presented itself at once. How to reveal the 1968 bugging without at the same time revealing what that bugging had been about? Hence the second thoughts ("that wasn't such a good idea . . ."). In his excellent introduction to *The Haldeman Diaries*, Nixon's biographer Professor Stephen Ambrose characterizes the 1973 approach to Lyndon Johnson as "prospective blackmail," designed to exert backstairs pressure to close down a congressional inquiry. But he also suggests that Johnson, himself no pushover, had some blackmail ammunition of his own. As Professor Ambrose phrases it, the Haldeman *Diaries* had been vetted by the National Security Council (NSC), and the bracketed deletion cited above is "the only place in the book where an example is given of a deletion by the NSC during the Carter administration. Eight days later Nixon was inaugurated for his second term. Ten days later Johnson died of a heart attack. What Johnson had on Nixon I suppose we'll never know."

The professor's conclusion here is arguably too tentative. There is a well-understood principle known as "Mutual Assured Destruction," whereby both sides possess more than enough material with which to annihilate the other. The answer to the question of what the Johnson administration "had" on Nixon is a relatively easy one. It was given in a book entitled *Counsel to the President*, published in 1991. Its author was Clark Clifford, the quintessential blue-chip Washington insider, who was assisted in the writing by Richard Holbrooke, the former Assistant Secretary of State and Ambassador to the United Nations. In 1968, Clark Clifford was Secretary of Defense and Richard Holbrooke was a member of the United States negotiating team at the Vietnam peace talks in Paris.

From his seat in the Pentagon, Clifford had actually been able to read the intelligence transcripts that picked up and recorded what he terms a "secret personal channel" between President Thieu in Saigon and the

Nixon campaign. The chief interlocutor at the American end was John Mitchell, then Nixon's campaign manager and subsequently Attorney General (and subsequently Prisoner Number 24171-157 in the Alabama correctional system). He was actively assisted by Madame Anna Chennault, known to all as The Dragon Lady. A fierce veteran of the Taiwan lobby, and all-purpose right-wing intriguer, she was a social and political force in the Washington of her day and would rate a biography on her own.

Clifford describes a private meeting at which he, President Johnson, Secretary of State Dean Rusk, and National Security Advisor Walt Rostow were present. Hawkish to a man, they kept Vice-President Humphrey out of the loop. But, hawkish as they were, they were appalled at the evidence of Nixon's treachery. They nonetheless decided not to go public with what they knew. Clifford says that this was because the disclosure would have ruined the Paris talks altogether. He could have added that it would have created a crisis of public confidence in United States institutions. There are some things that the voters can't be trusted to know. And, even though the bugging had been legal, it might not have looked like fair play. (The Logan Act prohibits any American from conducting private diplomacy with a foreign power, but it is not very rigorously or consistently enforced.)

In the event, Thieu pulled out of the negotiations anyway, ruining them just two days before the election. Clifford is in no doubt of the advice on which he did so:

> The activities of the Nixon team went far beyond the bounds of justifiable political combat. It constituted direct interference in the activities of the executive branch and the responsibilities of the Chief Executive, the only people with authority to negotiate on behalf of the nation. The activities of the Nixon campaign constituted a gross, even potentially illegal, interference in the security affairs of the nation by private individuals.

Perhaps aware of the slight feebleness of his lawyerly prose, and perhaps a little ashamed of keeping the secret for his memoirs rather than sharing it with the electorate, Clifford adds in a footnote:

It should be remembered that the public was considerably more innocent in such matters in the days before the Watergate hearings and the 1975 Senate investigation of the CIA.

Perhaps the public was indeed more innocent, if only because of the insider reticence of white-shoe lawyers like Clifford, who thought there were some things too profane to be made known. He claims now that he was in favor either of confronting Nixon privately with the information and forcing him to desist, or else of making it public. Perhaps this was indeed his view.

A more wised-up age of investigative reporting has brought us several updates on this appalling episode. And so has the very guarded memoir of Richard Nixon himself. More than one "back channel" was required for the Republican destabilization of the Paris peace talks. There had to be secret communications between Nixon and the South Vietnamese, as we have seen. But there also had to be an informant inside the incumbent administration's camp – a source of hints and tips and early warnings of official intentions. That informant was Henry Kissinger. In Nixon's own account, *RN: The Memoirs of Richard Nixon*, the disgraced elder statesman tells us that, in mid-September 1968, he received private word of a planned "bombing halt." In other words, the Johnson administration would, for the sake of the negotiations, consider suspending its aerial bombardment of North Vietnam. This most useful advance intelligence, Nixon tells us, came "through a highly unusual channel." It was more unusual even than he acknowledged. Kissinger had until then been a devoted partisan of Nelson Rockefeller, the matchlessly wealthy prince of liberal Republicanism. His contempt for the person and the policies of Richard Nixon was undisguised. Indeed, President Johnson's Paris negotiators, led by Averell Harriman, considered Kissinger to be almost one of themselves. He had made himself helpful, as Rockefeller's chief foreign policy advisor, by supplying French intermediaries with their own contacts in Hanoi. "Henry was the only person outside of the government we were authorised to discuss the negotiations with," says Richard Holbrooke. "We trusted him. It is not stretching the truth to say that the Nixon campaign had a secret source within the US negotiating team."

So the likelihood of a bombing halt, wrote Nixon, "came as no real surprise to me." He added: "I told Haldeman that Mitchell should continue as liaison with Kissinger and that we should honor his desire to keep his role completely confidential." It is impossible that Nixon was unaware of his campaign manager's parallel role in colluding with a foreign power. Thus began what was effectively a domestic covert operation, directed simultaneously at the thwarting of the talks and the embarrassment of the Hubert Humphrey campaign.

Later in the month, on 26 September to be precise, and as recorded by Nixon in his memoirs, "Kissinger called again. He said that he had just returned from Paris, where he had picked up word that something big was afoot regarding Vietnam. He advised that if I had anything to say about Vietnam during the following week, I should avoid any new ideas or proposals." On the same day, Nixon declined a challenge from Humphrey for a direct debate. On 12 October, Kissinger once again made contact, suggesting that a bombing halt might be announced as soon as 23 October. *And so it might have been.* Except that for some reason, every time the North Vietnamese side came closer to agreement, the South Vietnamese increased their own demands. We now know why and how that was, and how the two halves of the strategy were knit together. As far back as July, Nixon had met quietly in New York with the South Vietnamese ambassador, Bui Diem. The contact had been arranged by Anna Chennault. Bugging of the South Vietnamese offices in Washington, and surveillance of the Dragon Lady, showed how the ratchet operated. An intercepted cable from Diem to President Thieu on the fateful day of 23 October had him saying: "Many Republican friends have contacted me and encouraged us to stand firm. They were alarmed by press reports to the effect that you had already softened your position." The wiretapping instructions went to one Cartha De Loach, known as Deke to his associates, who was J. Edgar

Hoover's FBI liaison officer to the White House. We met him, you may recall, in H.R. Haldeman's *Diaries*.

In 1999 the author Anthony Summers was finally able to gain access to the closed FBI file of intercepts of the Nixon campaign, which he published in his 2000 book *The Arrogance of Power: The Secret World of Richard Nixon*. He was also able to interview Anna Chennault. These two breakthroughs furnished him with what is vulgarly termed a "smoking gun" on the 1968 conspiracy. By the end of October 1968, John Mitchell had become so nervous about official surveillance that he ceased taking calls from Chennault. And President Johnson, in a conference call to the three candidates, Nixon, Humphrey and Wallace (allegedly to brief them on the bombing halt), had strongly implied that he knew about the covert efforts to stymie his Vietnam diplomacy. This call created near-panic in Nixon's inner circle and caused Mitchell to telephone Chennault at the Sheraton Park Hotel. He then asked her to call him back on a more secure line. "Anna," he told her, "I'm speaking on behalf of Mr Nixon. It's very important that our Vietnamese friends understand our Republican position, and I hope you made that clear to them. . . . Do you think they really have decided not to go to Paris?"

The reproduced FBI original document shows what happened next. On 2 November 1968, the agent reported as follows:

MRS ANNA CHENNAULT CONTACTED VIETNAMESE AMBASSADOR BUI DIEM, AND ADVISED HIM THAT SHE HAD RECEIVED A MESSAGE FROM HER BOSS (NOT FURTHER IDENTIFIED), WHICH HER BOSS WANTED HER TO GIVE PERSONALLY TO THE AMBASSADOR. SHE SAID THAT THE MESSAGE WAS THAT THE AMBASSADOR IS TO "HOLD ON, WE ARE GONNA WIN" AND THAT HER BOSS ALSO SAID "HOLD ON, HE UNDERSTANDS ALL OF IT." SHE REPEATED THAT THIS IS THE ONLY MESSAGE. "HE SAID PLEASE TELL YOUR BOSS TO HOLD ON." SHE ADVISED THAT HER BOSS HAD JUST CALLED FROM NEW MEXICO.

Nixon's running mate, Spiro Agnew, had been campaigning in Albuquerque, New Mexico, that day, and subsequent intelligence analysis revealed that he, and another member of his staff (the one principally concerned with Vietnam), had indeed been in touch with the Chennault camp.

The beauty of having Kissinger leaking from one side, and Anna Chennault and John Mitchell conducting a private foreign policy for Nixon on the other, was this. It enabled him to avoid being drawn into the argument over a bombing halt. And it further enabled him to suggest that it was the Democrats who were playing politics with the issue. On 25 October in New York, Nixon used his tried-and-tested tactic of circulating an innuendo while purporting to disown it. Of LBJ's Paris diplomacy he said, "I am told that this spurt of activity is a cynical, last-minute attempt by President Johnson to salvage the candidacy of Mr Humphrey. This I do not believe."

Kissinger himself showed a similar ability to play both ends against the middle. In the late summer of 1968, on Martha's Vineyard, he had offered Nelson Rockefeller's files on Nixon to Professor Samuel Huntington, a close advisor to Hubert Humphrey. But when Huntington's colleague and friend Zbigniew Brzezinski tried to get him to make good on the offer, Kissinger became shy. "I've hated Nixon for years," he told Brzezinski. But the time wasn't quite ripe for the handover. Indeed, it was a very close-run election, turning in the end on a difference of a few hundred thousand votes, and many hardened observers believe that the final difference was made when Johnson ordered a bombing halt on 31 October and the South Vietnamese made him look a fool by boycotting the peace talks the very next day. But had things gone the other way, Kissinger was a near-certainty for a senior job in a Humphrey administration.

With slight differences of emphasis, the larger pieces of this story appear in Haldeman's work as cited, and in Clifford's memoir. They are also partially rehearsed in President Johnson's autobiography *The Vantage Point*, and in a long reflection on Indochina by William Bundy (one of the architects of the war) entitled rather tritely *The Tangled Web*. Senior members of the press corps, among them Jules Witcover in his history of 1968, Seymour Hersh in his study of Kissinger, and Walter Isaacson, editor of *Time* magazine, in his admiring but critical biography, have produced almost congruent accounts of the same abysmal episode. I myself parsed *The Haldeman Diaries* in *The Nation* in 1994. The only mention of it that is completely and utterly false, and false by any literary or historical standard, appears in the memoirs of Henry Kissinger himself. He writes just this:

> Several Nixon emissaries – some self-appointed – telephoned me for counsel. I took the position that I would answer specific questions on foreign policy, but that I would not offer general advice or volunteer suggestions. This was the same response I made to inquiries from the Humphrey staff.

This contradicts even the self-serving memoir of the man who, having won the 1968 election by these underhand means, made *as his very first appointment* Henry Kissinger as National Security Advisor. One might not want to arbitrate a mendacity competition between the two men, but when he made this choice Richard Nixon had only once, briefly and awkwardly, met Henry Kissinger in person. He clearly formed his estimate of the man's abilities from more persuasive experience than that. "One factor that had most convinced me of Kissinger's credibility," Nixon wrote later in his own delicious prose, "was the length to which he went to protect his secrecy."

But that ghastly secret is now out. In the December 1968 issue of the establishment house organ *Foreign Affairs*, written months earlier but published a few days after his gazetting as Nixon's right-hand man, there appeared Henry Kissinger's own evaluation of the Vietnam negotiations. On every point of substance, he agreed with the line taken in Paris by the Johnson–Humphrey negotiators. One has to pause for an instant to comprehend the enormity of this. Kissinger had helped elect a man who had surreptitiously promised the South Vietnamese junta a better deal than they would get from the Democrats. The Saigon authorities then acted, as Bundy ruefully confirms, as if they did indeed have a deal. This meant, in the words of a later Nixon slogan, "Four More Years." But four more years of an unwinnable and undeclared and murderous war, which was to spread before it burned out, and was to end on the same terms and conditions as had been on the table in the fall of 1968.

This was what it took to promote Henry Kissinger. To promote him from being a mediocre and opportunist academic to becoming an international potentate. The signature qualities were there from the inaugural moment: the sycophancy and the duplicity; the power worship and the absence of scruple; the empty trading of old non-friends for new non-friends. And the distinctive effects were also present: the uncounted and expendable corpses; the official and unofficial lying about the cost; the heavy and pompous pseudo-indignation when unwelcome questions were asked. Kissinger's global career started as it meant to go on. It debauched the American republic and American democracy, and it levied a hideous toll of casualties on weaker and more vulnerable societies.

BY WAY OF WARNING:
A BRIEF NOTE ON THE 40 COMMITTEE

In many of the ensuing pages and episodes, I've found it essential to allude to the "40 Committee" or the "Forty Committee," the semi-clandestine body of which Henry Kissinger was the chairman between 1969 and 1976. One does not need to picture some giant, octopuslike organization at the center of a web of conspiracy: however, it is important to know that there was a committee which maintained ultimate supervision over United States covert actions overseas (and, possibly, at home) during this period.

The CIA was originally set up by President Harry Truman at the beginning of the Cold War. In the first Eisenhower administration, it was felt necessary to establish a monitoring or watchdog body to oversee covert operations. This panel was known as the Special Group, and sometimes also referred to as the 54/12 Group, after the number of the National Security Council directive which set it up. By the time of President Johnson it was called the 303 Committee and during the Nixon and Ford administrations it was called the 40 Committee. Some believe that these changes of name reflect the numbers of later NSC directives; in fact the committee was known by the numbers of the successive rooms in the handsome Old Executive Office Building (now annexed to the neighboring White House) which used to shelter the three departments of "State, War and Navy," in which it met. No mystery there.

If any fantastic rumors shroud the work of the committee, this may be the outcome of the absurd cult of secrecy that at one point surrounded it. At Senate hearings in 1973, Senator Stuart Symington was questioning William Colby, then Director of Central Intelligence, about the origins and evolution of the supervisory group:

Senator Symington: Very well. What is the name of the latest committee of this character?

Mr Colby: Forty Committee.

Senator Symington: Who is the chairman?

Mr Colby: Well, again, I would prefer to go into executive session on the description of the Forty Committee, Mr Chairman.

Senator Symington: As to who is the chairman, you would prefer an executive session?

Mr Colby: The chairman – all right, Mr Chairman – Dr Kissinger is the chairman, as the Assistant to the President for National Security Affairs.

Kissinger held this position *ex officio*, in other words. His colleagues at the time were Air Force General George Brown, chairman of the Joint Chiefs of Staff; William P. Clements, Jr, the Deputy Secretary of Defense; Joseph Sisco, the Under-Secretary of State for Political Affairs; and the Director of Central Intelligence, William Colby.

With slight variations, those holding these positions have been the permanent members of the Forty Committee which, as President Ford phrased it in the first public reference by a president to the group's existence, "reviews every covert operation undertaken by our government." An important variation was added by President Nixon, who appointed his former campaign manager and attorney general, John Mitchell, to sit on the committee, the only attorney general to have done so. The founding charter of the CIA prohibits it from taking any part in domestic operations:

in January 1975 Attorney General Mitchell was convicted of numerous counts of perjury, obstruction and conspiracy to cover up the Watergate burglary, which was carried out in part by former CIA operatives. He became the first attorney general to serve time in jail.

We have met Mr Mitchell, in concert with Mr Kissinger, before. The usefulness of this note, I hope and believe, is that it supplies a thread which will be found throughout this narrative. Whenever any major US covert undertaking occurred between the years 1969 and 1976, Henry Kissinger may be at least presumed to have had direct knowledge of, and responsibility for, it. If he claims that he did not, then he is claiming not to have been doing a job to which he clung with great bureaucratic tenacity. And, whether or not he cares to accept the responsibility, the accountability is his in any case.

2

INDOCHINA

EVEN WHILE COMPELLED to concentrate on brute realities, one must never lose sight of that element of the surreal that surrounds Henry Kissinger. Paying a visit to Vietnam in the middle 1960s, when many technocratic opportunists were still convinced that the war was worth fighting and could be won, the young Henry reserved judgment on the first point but developed considerable private doubts on the second. Empowered by Nelson Rockefeller with a virtual free hand to develop contacts of his own, he had gone so far as to involve himself with an initiative that extended to direct personal contact with Hanoi. He became friendly with two Frenchmen who had a direct line to the Communist leadership in North Vietnam's capital. Raymond Aubrac, a French civil servant who was a friend of Ho Chi Minh, made common cause with Herbert Marcovich, a French biochemist, and began a series of trips to North Vietnam. On their return, they briefed Kissinger in Paris. He in his turn parlayed their information into high-level conversations in Washington, relaying the actual or potential negotiating positions of Pham Van Dong and other Communist statesmen to Robert McNamara. (In the result, the relentless bombing of the North made any "bridge-building" impracticable. In particular, the now-forgotten American destruction of the Paul Doumer bridge outraged the Vietnamese side.)

This weightless mid-position, which ultimately helped enable his double act in 1968, allowed Kissinger to ventriloquize Governor Rockefeller and to propose, by indirect means, a future détente with America's chief rivals. In his first major address as a candidate for the Republican nomination in 1968, Rockefeller spoke ringingly of how "in a subtle triangle with Communist China and the Soviet Union, we can ultimately improve our relations with *each* – as we test the will for peace of *both*." This foreshadowing of a later Kissinger strategy might appear at first reading to illustrate prescience. But Governor Rockefeller had no more reason than Vice-President Humphrey to suppose that his ambitious staffer would defect to the Nixon camp, risking and postponing this same détente in order later to take credit for a debased simulacrum of it.

Morally speaking, Kissinger treated the concept of superpower rapprochement in the same way as he treated the concept of a negotiated settlement in Vietnam: as something contingent to his own needs. There was a time to feign support of it, and a time to denounce it as weak-minded and treacherous. And there was a time to take credit for it. Some of those who "followed orders" in Indochina may lay a claim to that notoriously weak defense. Some who even issued the orders may now tell us that they were acting sincerely at the time. But Kissinger cannot avail himself of this alibi. He always knew what he was doing, and he embarked upon a second round of protracted warfare having knowingly helped to destroy an alternative which he always understood was possible. This increases the gravity of the charge against him. It also prepares us for his improvised and retrospective defense against that charge – that his immense depredations eventually led to "peace." When he falsely and prematurely announced that "peace is now at hand" in October 1972, he made a boastful claim that could have been genuinely (and much less bloodily) made in 1967. And when he claimed credit for subsequent superpower contacts, he was announcing the result of a secret and corrupt diplomacy that had originally been proposed as an open and democratic one. In the meantime, he had illegally eavesdropped and shadowed American citizens and public servants whose misgivings about the war, and about unconstitutional authority, were mild compared to those of Messieurs Aubrac and Marcovich. In establishing what lawyers call the *mens rea*, we can say that in Kissinger's case he was fully aware of, and is entirely accountable for, his own actions.

Upon taking office at Richard Nixon's side in the winter of 1968, it was Kissinger's task to be *plus royaliste que le roi* in two respects. He had to confect a rationale of "credibility" for punitive action in an already devastated Vietnamese theatre, and he had to second his principal's wish that he form part of a "wall" between the Nixon White House and the Department of State. The term "two-track" was later to become commonplace. Kissinger's position on both tracks, of promiscuous violence abroad and flagrant illegality at home, was decided from the start. He does not seem to have lacked relish for either commitment; one hopes faintly that this was not the first twinge of the "aphrodisiac."

President Johnson's "bombing halt" had not lasted long by any standards, even if one remembers that its original conciliatory purpose had been sordidly undercut. Averell Harriman, who had been LBJ's chief negotiator in Paris, later testified to Congress that the North Vietnamese had withdrawn 90 percent of their forces from the northern two provinces of South Vietnam, in October–November 1968, in accordance with the agreement of which the halt might have formed a part. In the new context, however, this withdrawal could be interpreted as a sign of weakness, or even as a "light at the end of the tunnel."

The historical record of the Indochina war is voluminous, and the resulting controversy no less so. However, this does not prevent the following of a consistent thread. Once the war had been unnaturally and undemocratically prolonged, more exorbitant methods were required to fight it and more fantastic excuses had to be fabricated to justify it. Let us take four separate but connected cases in which the civilian population was deliberately exposed to indiscriminate lethal force, in which the customary laws of war and neutrality were violated, and in which conscious lies had to be told in order to conceal these facts, and others.

The first such case is an example of what Vietnam might have been spared had not the 1968 Paris peace talks been sabotaged. In December 1968, during the "transition" period between the Johnson and Nixon administrations, the United States military command turned to what General Creighton Abrams termed "total war" against the "infrastructure" of the Vietcong/NLF insurgency. The chief exhibit in this campaign was a six-month clearance of the Mekong Delta province of Kien Hoa. The code name for the sweep was Operation Speedy Express. (See pages 30–33.)

It might, in some realm of theory, be remotely conceivable that such tactics could be justified under the international laws and charters governing the sovereign rights of self-defense. But no nation capable of deploying the overwhelming and annihilating force described below would be likely to find itself on the defensive. And it would be least of all likely to find itself on the defensive on its own soil. So the Nixon–Kissinger administration was not, except in one unusual sense, fighting for survival. The unusual sense in which its survival *was* at stake is set out, yet again, in the stark posthumous testimony of H.R. Haldeman. From his roost at Nixon's side he describes a Kissingerian moment on 15 December 1970:

> K[issinger] came in and the discussion covered some of the general thinking about Vietnam and the P's big peace plan for next year, which K later told me he does not favor. He thinks that any pullout next year would be a serious mistake because the adverse reaction to it could set in well before the '72 elections. He favors instead a continued winding down and then a pullout right at the fall of '72 so that if any bad results follow they will be too late to affect the election.

One could hardly wish for it to be more plainly put than that. (And put, furthermore, by one of Nixon's chief partisans with no wish to discredit the re-election.) But in point of fact Kissinger himself admits to almost as much in his own first volume of memoirs, *The White House Years*. The context is a meeting with General de Gaulle in which the old warrior demanded to know by what right the Nixon administration subjected

Indochina to devastating bombardment. In his own account, Kissinger replies that "a sudden withdrawal might give us a credibility problem." (When asked "Where?", Kissinger hazily proposed the Middle East.) It is important to bear in mind that the future flatterer of Brezhnev and Mao, and the proponent of the manipulative "triangle" between them, was in no real position to claim that he made war in Indochina to thwart either. He certainly did not dare try such a callow excuse on Charles de Gaulle. And indeed, the proponent of secret deals with China was in no very strong position to claim that he was combating Stalinism in general. No, it all came down to "credibility," and to the saving of face. It is known that 20,492 American servicemen lost their lives in Indochina between the day that Nixon and Kissinger took office and the day in 1972 that they withdrew United States forces and accepted the logic of 1968. What if the families and survivors of these victims have to confront the fact that the "face" at risk was Kissinger's own?

Thus the colloquially entitled "Christmas bombing" of North Vietnam, begun during the same election campaign that Haldeman and Kissinger had so tenderly foreseen two years previously, and continued after that election had been won, must be counted as a war crime by any standard. The bombing was not conducted for anything that could be described as "military reasons," but for twofold political reasons. The first of these was domestic: to make a show of strength to extremists in Congress and to put the Democratic Party on the defensive. The second reason was to persuade the South Vietnamese leaders like President Thieu – still intransigent after all those years – that their objections to a United States withdrawal were too nervous. This, again, was the mortgage on the initial secret payment of 1968.

When the unpreventable collapse occurred, in Vietnam and in Cambodia, in April and May 1975, the cost was infinitely higher than it would have been seven years previously. These locust years ended as they had begun – with a display of bravado and deceit. On 12 May 1975, Cambodian gunboats detained an American merchant vessel named the *Mayaguez*. In the immediate aftermath of the Khmer Rouge seizure of power, the situation was a distraught one. The ship had been stopped in international waters claimed by Cambodia and then taken to the Cambodian island of Koh Tang. In spite of reports that the crew had been released, Kissinger pressed for an immediate face-saving and "credibility"-enhancing strike. He persuaded President Gerald Ford, the untried and undistinguished successor to his deposed former boss, to send in the Marines and the Air Force. Out of a Marine force of 110, 18 were killed and 50 wounded. Some 23 Air Force men died in a crash. The United States used a 15,000-pound bomb on the island, the most powerful non-nuclear device that it possessed. Nobody has the figures for Cambodian deaths. The casualties were pointless because the ship's company of the *Mayaguez* were nowhere on Koh Tang, having been released some hours earlier. A subsequent congressional inquiry found that Kissinger could have known of this by listening to Cambodian Broadcasting or by paying attention to a third-party government which had been negotiating a deal for the restitution of the crew and the ship. It was not as if any Cambodians doubted, by that month of 1975, the willingness of the US government to employ deadly force.

In Washington, DC, there is a famous and hallowed memorial to the American dead of the Vietnam War. Known as the Vietnam Veterans' Memorial, it bears a name that is slightly misleading. I was present for the extremely affecting moment of its dedication in 1982, and noticed that the list of nearly 60,000 names is incised in the wall not by alphabet but by date. The first few names appear in 1954, and the last few in 1975. The more historically minded visitors can sometimes be heard to say that they didn't know the United States was engaged in Vietnam as early or as late as that. Nor were the public supposed to know. The first names are of the covert operatives sent in by Colonel Lansdale without congressional approval to support French colonialism before Dien Bien Phu. The last names are of those thrown away in the *Mayaguez* fiasco. It took Henry Kissinger to ensure that a war of atrocity, which he had helped prolong, should end as furtively and ignominiously as it had begun.

3

A SAMPLE OF CASES:
KISSINGER'S WAR CRIMES IN INDOCHINA

SOME STATEMENTS ARE too blunt for everyday, consensual discourse. In national "debate," it is the smoother pebbles that are customarily gathered from the stream, and used as projectiles. They leave less of a scar, even when they hit. Occasionally, however, a single hard-edged remark will inflict a deep and jagged wound, a gash so ugly that it must be cauterized at once. In January 1971, General Telford Taylor, who had been chief prosecuting counsel at the Nuremberg trials, made a considered statement. Reviewing the legal and moral basis of those hearings, and also the Tokyo trials of Japanese war criminals and the Manila trial of Emperor Hirohito's chief militarist, General Tomoyuki Yamashita, Taylor said that if the standards of Nuremberg and Manila were applied evenly, and applied to the American statesmen and bureaucrats who designed the war in Vietnam, then "there would be a very strong possibility that they would come to the same end he [Yamashita] did." It is not every day that a senior American soldier and jurist delivers the opinion that a large portion of his country's political class should probably be hooded and blindfolded and dropped through a trapdoor on the end of a rope.

In his book *Nuremberg and Vietnam*, General Taylor also anticipated one of the possible objections to this legal and moral conclusion. It might be argued for the defense, he said, that those arraigned did not really know what they were doing; in other words had achieved the foulest results but from the highest and most innocent motives. The notion of Indochina as some *Heart of Darkness* "quagmire" of ignorant armies has been sedulously propagated, then and since, but Taylor had no patience with such a view. American military and intelligence and economic and political missions and teams had been in Vietnam, he wrote, for much too long to attribute anything they did "to lack of information." It might have been possible for soldiers and diplomats to pose as innocents until the middle of the 1960s, but after that time, and especially after the My Lai massacre of 16 March 1968, when serving veterans reported to their superior officers a number of major atrocities, nobody could reasonably claim to have been uninformed and of those who could, the least believable would be those who – far from the confusion of battle – read and discussed and approved the panoptic reports of the war that were delivered to Washington.

General Taylor's book was being written while many of the most reprehensible events of the Indochina war were still taking place, or were still to come. He was unaware of the intensity and extent of, for example, the bombing of Laos and Cambodia. However, enough was known about the conduct of the war, and about the existing matrix of legal and criminal responsibility, for him to arrive at some indisputable conclusions. The first of these concerned the particular obligation of the United States to be aware of, and to respect, the Nuremberg principles:

> Military courts and commissions have customarily rendered their judgments stark and unsupported by opinions giving the reason for their decision. The Nuremberg and Tokyo judgments, in contrast, were all based on extensive opinions detailing the evidence and analyzing the factual and legal issues, in the fashion of appellate tribunals generally. Needless to say they were not of uniform quality, and often reflected the logical shortcomings of compromise, the marks of which commonly mar the opinions of multi-member tribunals. But the process was *professional* in a way seldom achieved in military courts, and the records and judgments in these trials

provided a much-needed foundation for a corpus of judge-made international penal law. The results of the trials commended themselves to the newly-formed United Nations, and on December 11, 1946, the General Assembly adopted a resolution affirming "the principles of international law recognized by the Charter of the Nuremberg Tribunal and the judgment of the Tribunal."

However history may ultimately assess the wisdom or unwisdom of the war crimes trials, one thing is indisputable. At their conclusion, the United States Government stood legally, politically and morally committed to the principles enunciated in the charters and judgments of the tribunals. The President of the United States, on the recommendations of the Departments of State, War and Justice, approved the war crimes programs. Thirty or more American judges, drawn from the appellate benches of the states from Massachusetts to Oregon, and Minnesota to Georgia, conducted the later Nuremberg trials and wrote the opinions. General Douglas MacArthur, under authority of the Far Eastern Commission, established the Tokyo tribunal and confirmed the sentences it imposed, and it was under his authority as the highest American military officer in the Far East that the Yamashita and other such proceedings were held. The United States delegation to the United Nations presented the resolution by which the General Assembly endorsed the Nuremberg principles. Thus the integrity of the nation is staked on those principles, and today the question is how they apply to our conduct of the war in Vietnam, and whether the United States Government is prepared to face the consequences of their application.

Facing and cogitating these consequences himself, General Telford Taylor took issue with another United States officer, Colonel William Corson, who had written that "Regardless of the outcome of . . . the My Lai courts-martial and other legal actions, the point remains that American judgment as to the effective prosecution of the war was faulty from beginning to end and that the atrocities, alleged or otherwise, are a result of failure of judgment, not criminal behavior." To this Telford responded thus:

Colonel Corson overlooks, I fear, that negligent homicide is generally a crime of bad judgment rather than evil intent. Perhaps he is right in the strictly causal sense that if there had been no failure of judgment, the occasion for criminal conduct would not have arisen. The Germans in occupied Europe made gross errors of judgment which no doubt created the conditions in which the slaughter of the inhabitants of Klissura [a Greek village annihilated during the Occupation] occurred, but that did not make the killings any the less criminal.

Referring this question to the chain of command in the field, General Taylor noted further that the senior officer corps had been:

more or less constantly in Vietnam, and splendidly equipped with helicopters and other aircraft, which gave them a degree of mobility unprecedented in earlier wars, and consequently endowed them with every opportunity to keep the course of the fighting and its consequences under close and constant observation. Communications were generally rapid and efficient, so that the flow of information and orders was unimpeded.

These circumstances are in sharp contrast to those that confronted General Yamashita in 1944 and 1945, with his troops reeling back in disarray before the oncoming American military powerhouse. For failure to control his troops so as to prevent the atrocities they committed, Brigadier Generals Egbert F. Bullene and Morris Handwerk and Major Generals James A. Lester, Leo Donovan and Russel B. Reynolds found him guilty of violating the laws of war and sentenced him to death by hanging.

Nor did General Taylor omit the crucial link between the military command and its political supervision; this was again a much closer and more immediate relation in the American–Vietnamese instance than in the Japanese–Filipino one, as the regular contact between, say, General Creighton Abrams and Henry Kissinger makes clear:

How much the President and his close advisors in the White House, Pentagon and Foggy Bottom knew about the volume and cause of civilian casualties in Vietnam, and the physical devastation of the countryside, is speculative. Something was known, for the late John Naughton (then Assistant Secretary of Defense) returned from the White House one day in 1967 with the message that "We seem to be proceeding on the assumption that the way to eradicate the Vietcong is to destroy all the village structures, defoliate all the jungles, and then cover the entire surface of South Vietnam with asphalt."

This remark had been reported (by Townsend Hoopes, a political antagonist of General Taylor) before that metaphor had been extended into two new countries, Laos and Cambodia, without a declaration of war, a notification to Congress, or a warning to civilians to evacuate. But Taylor anticipated the Kissinger case in many ways when he recalled the trial of the Japanese statesman Koki Hirota:

> who served briefly as Prime Minister and for several years as Foreign Minister between 1933 and May 1938, after which he held no office whatever. The so-called "Rape of Nanking" by Japanese forces occurred during the winter of 1937–38, when Hirota was Foreign Minister. Upon receiving early reports of the atrocities, he demanded and received assurances from the War Ministry that they would be stopped. But they continued, and the Tokyo tribunal found Hirota guilty because he was "derelict in his duty in not insisting before the Cabinet that immediate action be taken to put an end to the atrocities," and "was content to rely on assurances which he knew were not being implemented." On this basis, coupled with his conviction on the aggressive war charge, Hirota was sentenced to be hanged.

Melvin Laird, as Secretary of Defense during the first Nixon administration, was queasy enough about the early bombings of Cambodia, and dubious enough about the legality or prudence of the intervention, to send a memo to the Joint Chiefs of Staff, asking, "Are steps being taken, on a continuing basis, to minimize the risk of striking Cambodian peoples and structures. If so, what are the steps? Are we reasonably sure such steps are effective." There is no evidence of Henry Kissinger, as National Security Advisor or Secretary of State, ever seeking even such modest assurances. Indeed, there is much evidence of his deceiving Congress about the true extent to which such assurances as were offered were deliberately false. Others involved, like Robert McNamara, McGeorge Bundy and William

Colby, have since offered varieties of apology or contrition or at least explanation: Henry Kissinger never. General Taylor described the practise of air strikes against hamlets suspected of "harboring" Vietnamese guerrillas as "flagrant violations of the Geneva Convention on Civilian Protection, which prohibits 'collective penalties' and 'reprisals against protected persons' and equally in violation of the Rules of Land Warfare." He was writing before this atrocious precedent had been extended to "reprisal raids" that treated two whole countries – Laos and Cambodia – as if they were disposable hamlets.

For Henry Kissinger, no great believer in the boastful claims of the warmakers in the first place, a special degree of responsibility attaches. Not only did he have good reason to know that field commanders were exaggerating successes and claiming all dead bodies as enemy soldiers – a commonplace piece of knowledge after the spring of 1968 – but he also knew that the issue of the war had been settled politically and diplomatically, for all intents and purposes, before he became National Security Advisor. Thus he had to know that every additional casualty, on either side, was not just a death but an avoidable death. And with this knowledge, and with a strong sense of the domestic and personal political profit, he urged the expansion of the war into two neutral countries – violating international law – while persisting in a breathtakingly high level of attrition in Vietnam itself.

From a huge range of possible examples, I have chosen cases which involve Kissinger directly and in which I have myself been able to interview surviving witnesses. The first, as foreshadowed above, is Operation Speedy Express.

My friend and colleague Kevin Buckley, then a much-admired correspondent and Saigon bureau chief for *Newsweek*, became interested in the "pacification" campaign which bore this breezy code name. Designed in the closing days of the Johnson–Humphrey administration, it was put into full effect in the first six months of 1969, when Henry Kissinger had assumed much authority over the conduct of the war. The objective was the disciplining, on behalf of the Thieu government, of the turbulent Mekong Delta province of Kien Hoa.

On 22 January 1968, Defense Secretary Robert McNamara had told the Senate that "no regular North Vietnamese units" were deployed in the Mekong Delta, and no military intelligence documents have surfaced to undermine his claim, so that the cleansing of the area cannot be understood as part of the general argument about resisting Hanoi's unsleeping will to conquest. The announced purpose of the Ninth Division's sweep, indeed, was to redeem many thousands of villagers from political control by the National Liberation Front (NLF) or Viet Cong (VC). As Buckley found, and as his magazine *Newsweek* partially disclosed at the rather late date of 19 June 1972:

> All the evidence I gathered pointed to a clear conclusion: a staggering number of noncombatant civilians – perhaps as many as 5,000 according to one official – were killed by US firepower to "pacify" Kien Hoa. The death toll there made the My Lai massacre look trifling by comparison. . . .
>
> The Ninth Division put all it had into the operation. Eight thousand infantrymen scoured the heavily populated countryside, but contact with the elusive enemy was rare. Thus, in its pursuit of pacification, the division relied heavily on its 50 artillery pieces, 50 helicopters (many armed with rockets and mini-guns) and the deadly support lent by the Air Force. There were 3,381 tactical air strikes by fighter bombers during "Speedy Express." . . .
>
> "Death is our business and business is good," was the slogan painted on one helicopter unit's quarters during the operation. And so it was. Cumulative statistics for "Speedy Express" show that 10,899 "enemy" were killed. In the month of March alone, "over 3,000 enemy troops were killed . . . which is the largest monthly total for any American division in the Vietnam War," said the division's official magazine. When asked to account for the enormous body counts, a division senior officer explained that helicopter gun crews often caught unarmed "enemy" in open fields. . . .
>
> There is overwhelming evidence that virtually all the Viet Cong were well armed. Simple civilians were, of course, not armed. And the enormous discrepancy between the body count (11,000) and the number of captured weapons (748) is hard to explain – except by the conclusion that many victims were unarmed innocent civilians. . . .

The people who still live in pacified Kien Hoa all have vivid recollections of the devastation that American firepower brought to their lives in early 1969. Virtually every person to whom I spoke had suffered in some way. "There were 5,000 people in our village before 1969, but there were none in 1970," one village elder told me. "The Americans destroyed every house with artillery, air strikes, or by burning them down with cigarette lighters. About 100 people were killed by bombing, others were wounded and others became refugees. Many were children killed by concussion from the bombs which their small bodies could not withstand, even if they were hiding under-ground."

Other officials, including the village police chief, corroborated the man's testimony. I could not, of course, reach every village. But in each of the many places where I went, the testimony was the same: 100 killed here, 200 killed there.

Other notes by Buckley and his friend and collaborator Alex Shimkin (a worker for International Voluntary Services who was later killed in the war) discovered the same telltale evidence in hospital statistics. In March 1969, the hospital at Ben Tre reported 343 patients injured by "friendly fire" and 25 by "the enemy," an astonishing statistic for a government facility to record in a guerrilla war where suspected membership of the Viet Cong could mean death. And Buckley's own citation for his magazine – of "per-haps as many as 5,000 deaths" among civilians in this one sweep – is an almost deliberate understatement of what he was told by a United States official, who actually said that "*at least* 5,000" of the dead "were what we refer to as noncombatants": a not-too-exacting distinction, as we have already seen, and as was by then well understood (italics mine).

Well understood, that is to say, not just by those who opposed the war but by those who were conducting it. As one United States official put it to Buckley:

The actions of the Ninth Division in inflicting civilian casualties were worse [than My Lai]. The sum total of what the Ninth did was overwhelming. In sum, the horror was worse than My Lai. But with the Ninth, the civilian

casualties came in dribbles and were pieced out over a long time. And most
of them were inflicted from the air and at night. Also, they were sanctioned
by the command's insistence on high body-counts. . . . The result was an
inevitable outcome of the unit's command policy.

The earlier sweep which had mopped up My Lai – during Operation
Wheeler Wallawa – had also at the time counted all corpses as those of
enemy soldiers, including the civilian population of the village, who were
casually included in the mind-bending overall total of 10,000.

Confronted with this evidence, Buckley and Shimkin abandoned a lazy
and customary usage and replaced it, in a cable to *Newsweek* headquarters
in New York, with a more telling and scrupulous one. The problem was not
"indiscriminate use of firepower," but "charges of quite *discriminating* use –
as a matter of policy in populated areas." Even the former is a gross violation of the Geneva Convention; the second charge leads straight to the
dock in Nuremberg or The Hague.

Since General Creighton Abrams publicly praised the Ninth Division
for its work, and drew attention wherever and whenever he could to the
tremendous success of Operation Speedy Express, we can be sure that the
political leadership in Washington was not unaware. Indeed, the degree of
micro-management revealed in Kissinger's memoirs forbids the idea that
anything of importance took place without his knowledge or permission.

Of nothing is this more true than his own individual involvement in the
bombing and invasion of neutral Cambodia and Laos. Obsessed with the
idea that Vietnamese intransigence could be traced to allies or resources
external to Vietnam itself, or could be overcome by tactics of mass destruction, Kissinger at one point contemplated using thermonuclear weapons to
obliterate the pass through which ran the railway link from North Vietnam
to China, and at another stage considered bombing the dikes that prevented North Vietnam's irrigation system from flooding the country.
Neither of these measures (reported respectively in Tad Szulc's history of
Nixon-era diplomacy and by Kissinger's former aide Roger Morris) was

taken, which removes some potential war crimes from our bill of indictment but which also gives an indication of the regnant mentality. There
remained Cambodia and Laos, which supposedly concealed or protected
North Vietnamese supply lines.

As in the cases postulated by General Telford Taylor, there is the crime
of aggressive war and then there is the question of war crimes. (The Koki
Hirota case cited above is of importance here.) In the period after the
Second World War, or the period governed by the UN Charter and its
related and incorporated Conventions, the United States under Democratic
and Republican administrations had denied even its closest allies the right
to invade countries that allegedly gave shelter to their antagonists. Most
famously, President Eisenhower exerted economic and diplomatic pressure
at a high level to bring an end to the invasion of Egypt by Britain, France
and Israel in October 1956. (The British thought Nasser should not control
"their" Suez Canal; the French believed Nasser to be the inspiration and
source of their troubles in Algeria; and the Israelis claimed that he played
the same role in fomenting their difficulties with the Palestinians. The
United States maintained that even if these propaganda fantasies were true,
they would not retrospectively legalize an invasion of Egypt.) During the
Algerian war of independence, also, the United States had repudiated
France's claimed right to attack a town in neighboring Tunisia that suc-
coured Algerian guerrillas, and in 1964 Ambassador Adlai Stevenson at
the United Nations had condemned the United Kingdom for attacking a
town in Yemen that allegedly provided a rear guard for rebels operating in
its then colony of Aden.

All this law and precedent was to be thrown to the winds when Nixon
and Kissinger decided to aggrandize the notion of "hot pursuit" across the
borders of Laos and Cambodia. Even before the actual territorial invasion
of Cambodia, for example, and very soon after the accession of Nixon and
Kissinger to power, a program of heavy bombardment of the country was
prepared and executed in secret. One might with some revulsion call it a
"menu" of bombardment, since the code names for the raids were

"Breakfast," Lunch," "Snack," "Dinner," and "Dessert." The raids were flown by B-52 bombers which, it is important to note at the outset, fly at an altitude too high to be observed from the ground and carry immense tonnages of high explosive: they give no warning of approach and are incapable of accuracy or discrimination because of both their altitude and the mass of their shells. Between 18 March 1969 and May 1970, 3,630 such raids were flown across the Cambodian frontier. The bombing campaign began as it was to go on – with full knowledge of its effect on civilians, and with flagrant deceit by Mr Kissinger in this precise respect.

For example, a memorandum prepared by the Joint Chiefs of Staff and sent to the Defense Department and the White House said plainly that "some Cambodian casualties would be sustained in the operation" and "the surprise effect of attack could tend to increase casualties." The target district for Breakfast (Base Area 35) was inhabited, said the memo, by about 1,640 Cambodian civilians. Lunch (Base Area 609) was inihabited by 198 of them, Snack (Base Area 351) by 383, Dinner (Base Area 352) by 770, and Dessert (Base Area 350) by about 120 Cambodian peasants. These oddly exact figures are enough in themselves to demonstrate that Kissinger was lying when he later told the Senate Foreign Relations Committee that areas of Cambodia selected for bombing were "unpopulated."

As a result of the expanded and intensified bombing campaigns, it has been estimated that as many as 350,000 civilians in Laos, and 600,000 in Cambodia, lost their lives. (These are not the highest estimates.) Figures for refugees are several multiples of that. In addition, the widespread use of toxic chemical defoliants created a massive health crisis which naturally fell most heavily on children, nursing mothers, the aged and the already infirm, and which persists to this day.

Though this appalling war, and its appalling consequences, can and should be taken as a moral and political crisis for American institutions, for at least five United States presidents, and for American society, there is little difficulty in identifying individual responsibility during this, its most atrocious and indiscriminate stage. Richard Nixon as Commander in Chief bears ultimate responsibility, and only narrowly escaped a congressional move to include his crimes and deceptions in Indochina in the articles of impeachment, the promulgation of which eventually compelled his resignation. But his deputy and closest advisor, Henry Kissinger, was sometimes forced, and sometimes forced himself, into a position of virtual co-presidency where Indochina was concerned.

For example, in the preparations for the invasion of Cambodia in 1970, Kissinger was caught between the views of his staff – several of whom resigned in protest when the invasion began – and his need to please his President. His President listened more to his two criminal associates – John Mitchell and Bebe Rebozo – than he did to his Secretaries of State and Defense, William Rogers and Melvin Laird, both of whom were highly skeptical about widening the war. On one especially charming occasion, a drunken Nixon telephoned Kissinger to discuss the invasion plans. He then put Bebe Rebozo on the line. "The President wants you to know if this doesn't work, Henry, it's your ass." "Ain't that right, Bebe?" slurred the Commander in Chief. (The conversation was monitored and transcribed by one of Kissinger's soon-to-resign staffers, William Watts.[*]) It could be said that in this instance the National Security Advisor was under pressure; nevertheless he took the side of the pro-invasion faction and, according to the memoirs of General William Westmoreland, actually lobbied for that invasion to go ahead.

A somewhat harder picture is presented by former Chief of Staff H.R. Haldeman in his *Diaries*. On 22 December 1970, he records:

> Henry came up with the need to meet with the P[resident] today with Al Haig and then tomorrow with Laird and Moorer because he has to use the P[resident] to force Laird and the military to go ahead with the P[resident]'s plans, which they won't carry out without direct orders. The plans in question, involved . . . attacking enemy forces in Laos.

---

[*] According to Woodward and Bernstein, Watts then had a word with General Alexander Haig, who told him: "You've just had an order from your Commander in Chief. You can't resign." "Fuck you, Al," said Watts. "I just did."

In his own memoirs, *White House Years*, Kissinger claims that he usurped the customary chain of command whereby commanders in the field receive, or believe that they receive, their orders from the President and then the Secretary of Defense. He boasts that he, together with Haldeman, Alexander Haig and Colonel Ray Sitton, evolved "both a military and a diplomatic schedule" for the secret bombing of Cambodia. On board Air Force One, which was on the tarmac at Brussels airport on 24 February 1969, he writes, "we worked out the guidelines for the bombing of the enemy's sanctuaries." Air Force Colonel Sitton, the reigning expert on B-52 tactics at the Joint Chiefs of Staff, noted that the President was not at the meeting but had said that he would be discussing the subject with Kissinger. A few weeks later, Haldeman's *Diaries* for 17 March record:

> Historic day. K[issinger]'s "Operation Breakfast" finally came off at 2.00 PM our time. K[issinger] really excited, as was P[resident].

The next day's entry reads:

> K[issinger]'s "Operation Breakfast" a great success. He came beaming in with the report, very productive.

It only got better. On 22 April 1970, Haldeman reports that Nixon, following Kissinger into a National Security Council meeting on Cambodia, "turned back to me with a big smile and said 'K[issinger]'s really having fun today, he's playing Bismarck.'"

The above is an insult to the Iron Chancellor. When Kissinger was finally exposed in Congress and the press for conducting unauthorized bombings, he weakly pleaded that the raids were not all that secret, really, because Prince Sihanouk of Cambodia had known of them. He had to be reminded that a foreign princeling cannot give permission to an American bureaucrat to violate the United States Constitution. Nor, for the matter of that, can he give permission to an American bureaucrat to slaughter large numbers of his "own" civilians. It's difficult to imagine Bismarck cowering behind such a contemptible excuse. (Prince Sihanouk, it is worth remembering, later became an abject puppet of the Khmer Rouge.)

Colonel Sitton began to notice that by late 1969 his own office was being regularly overruled in the matter of selecting targets. "Not only was Henry carefully screening the raids," said Sitton, "he was reading the raw intelligence" and fiddling with the mission patterns and bombing runs. In other departments of Washington insiderdom, it was also noticed that Kissinger was becoming a Stakhanovite committeeman. Aside from the crucial Forty Committee, which planned and oversaw all foreign covert actions, he chaired the Washington Special Action Group (WSAG), the Verification Panel, which was concerned with arms control, the Vietnam Special Studies Group, which oversaw the day-to-day conduct of the war, and the Defense Program Review Committee, which supervised the budget of the Defense Department.

It is therefore impossible for him to claim that he was unaware of the consequences of the bombings of Cambodia and Laos; he knew more about them, and in more intimate detail, than any other individual. Nor was he imprisoned in a culture of obedience that gave him no alternative, or no rival arguments. Several senior members of his own staff, most notably Anthony Lake and Roger Morris, resigned over the invasion of Cambodia, and more than two hundred State Department employees signed a protest addressed to Secretary of State William Rogers. Indeed, as has been noted, both Rogers and Secretary of Defense Melvin Laird were opposed to the B-52 bombing policy, as Kissinger himself records with some disgust in his own memoirs. Congress was also opposed to an extension of the bombing (once it had agreed to become informed of it) but, even after the Nixon–Kissinger administration had undertaken on Capitol Hill not to intensify the raids, there was a 21 percent increase of the bombing of Cambodia in the months July–August 1973. The Air Force maps of the targeted areas show them to be, or to have been, densely populated.

Colonel Sitton does recall, it must be admitted, that Kissinger requested that bombing avoid civilian casualties. His explicit motive in making this request was to avoid or forestall complaints from the government of Prince Sihanouk. But this does no more in itself than demonstrate that Kissinger was aware of the possibility of civilian deaths. If he knew enough to know of their likelihood, and was director of the policy that inflicted them, and neither enforced any actual precautions nor reprimanded any violators, then the case against him is legally and morally complete.

As early as the fall of 1970, an independent investigator named Fred Branfman, who spoke Lao and knew the country as a civilian volunteer, had gone to Bangkok and interviewed Jerome Brown, a former targeting officer for the United States embassy in the Laotian capital of Vientiane. The man had retired from the Air Force because of his disillusionment at the futility of the bombing and his consternation at the damage done to civilians and society. The speed and height of the planes, he said, meant that targets were virtually indistinguishable from the air. Pilots would often decide to drop bombs where craters already existed, and chose villages as targets because they could be more readily identified than alleged Pathet Lao guerrillas hiding in the jungle. Branfman, whom I interviewed in San Francisco in the summer of 2000, went on to provide this and other information to Henry Kamm and Sydney Schanberg of the *New York Times*, to Ted Koppel of ABC, and to many others. He also wrote up and published his findings in *Harper's* magazine, where they were not controverted by any authority. Under pressure from the US embassy, the Laotian authorities had Branfman deported back to the United States, which was probably, from their point of view, a mistake. He was able to make a dramatic appearance on Capitol Hill on 22 April 1971, at a hearing held by Senator Edward Kennedy's Senate Subcommittee on Refugees. His antagonist was the State Department's envoy William Sullivan, a former ambassador to Laos. Branfman accused him in front of the cameras of helping to conceal evidence that Laotian society was being mutilated by ferocious aerial bombardment.

Partly as a consequence, Congressman Pete McCloskey of California (a much-decorated veteran of the war in Korea) paid a visit to Laos and acquired a copy of an internal US embassy study of the bombing. He also prevailed on the US Air Force to furnish him with aerial photographs of the dramatic damage. Ambassador Sullivan was so disturbed by these pictures, some of them taken in areas known to him, that his first reaction was to establish to his own satisfaction that the raids had occurred after he left his post in Vientiane. (He was later to learn that, for his pains, his own telephone was being tapped at Henry Kissinger's instigation, one of the many such violations of American law that were to eventuate in the Watergate tapping-and-burglary scandal: a scandal that Kissinger was furthermore to plead – in an astounding outburst of vanity, deceit and self-deceit – as his own alibi for inattention in the Cyprus crisis.)

Having done what he could to bring the Laotian nightmare to the attention of those whose constitutional job it was to supervise such questions, Branfman went back to Thailand and from there to Phnom Penh, capital of Cambodia. Having gained access to a pilot's radio, he tape-recorded the conversations between pilots on bombing missions over the Cambodian interior. On no occasion did they run any checks designed to reasssure themselves and others that they were not bombing civilian targets. It had been definitely asserted, by named US government spokesmen, that such checks were run. Branfman handed the tapes to Sydney Schanberg, whose *New York Times* report on them was printed just before the Senate met to prohibit further blitzing of Cambodia (the very resolution that was flouted by Kissinger the following month).

From there Branfman went back to Thailand and travelled north to Nakhorn Phanom, the new headquarters of the US Seventh Air Force. Here, a war room code-named "Blue Chip" served as the command and control center of the bombing campaign. Branfman, who is tall and well-built, was able to pose as a new recruit just up from Saigon, and ultimately to gain access to the war room itself. Here, consoles and maps and screens plotted the progress of the bombardment. In conversation with the "bombing officer" on duty, he asked if pilots ever made contact before dropping their enormous loads of ordnance. Oh, yes, he was assured, they did. Worried about hitting the innocent? Oh, no – merely concerned about the where-abouts of CIA "ground teams" infiltrated into the area. Branfman's report on this, which was carried by Jack Anderson's syndicated column and also in the *Washington Monthly*, was likewise uncontroverted by any official denial.

One reason that the United States command in Southeast Asia finally ceased employing the crude and horrific tally of "body count" was that, as in the relatively small but but specific case of Speedy Express cited above, the figures began to look ominous when they were counted up. Sometimes, totals of "enemy" dead would turn out, when computed, to be suspiciously larger than the number of claimed "enemy" in the field. Yet the war would somehow drag on, with new quantitative goals being set and enforced. Thus, according to the Pentagon, the following are the casualty figures between the first Lyndon Johnson bombing halt in March 1968 and the same date in 1972:

Americans	31,205
South Vietnamese regulars	86,101
"Enemy"	475,609

The US Senate Subcommittee on Refugees estimated that in the same four-year period rather more than three million civilians were killed, injured or rendered homeless. In the same four-year period, the United States dropped almost 4,500,000 tons of high explosive on Indochina. (The Pentagon's estimated total for the tonnage dropped in the entire Second World War is 2,044,000.) This total does not include massive sprayings of chemical defoliants and pesticides, the effects of which are still being registered by the region's ecology. Nor does it include the land-mines which detonate to this day.

It is unclear how we count the murder or abduction of 35,708 Vietnamese civilians by the CIA's counter-guerrilla "Phoenix program" during the first two and a half years of the Nixon–Kissinger administration. There may be some "overlap." There is also some overlap with the actions of previous administrations in all cases. But the truly exorbitant death tolls all occurred on Henry Kissinger's watch, were known and understood by him, were concealed from Congress, the press and the public by him – at any rate to the best of his ability – and were, when questioned, the subject of political and bureaucratic vendettas ordered by him. They were also partly the outcome of a secretive and illegal process in Washington, unknown even to most cabinet members, of which Henry Kissinger stood to be, and became, a prime beneficiary.

On that closing point one may once again cite H.R. Haldeman, who had no further reason to lie and who had, by the time of his writing, paid for his crimes by serving a sentence in prison. Haldeman describes the moment in Florida when Kissinger was enraged by a *New York Times* story telling some part of the truth about Indochina:

> Henry telephoned J. Edgar Hoover in Washington from Key Biscayne on the May morning the *Times* story appeared.
>
> According to Hoover's memo of the call, Henry said the story used "secret information which was extraordinarily damaging." Henry went on to tell Hoover that he "wondered whether I could make a major effort to find out where that came from . . . and to put whatever resources I need to find out who did this. I told him I would take care of this right away."
>
> Henry was no fool, of course. He telephoned Hoover a few hours later to remind him that the investigation be handled discreetly "so no stories will get out." Hoover must have smiled, but said all right. And by five o'clock he was back on the telephone to Henry with the report that the *Times* reporter "may have gotten some of his information from the Southeast Asian desk of the Department of Defense's Public Affairs Office." More specifically, Hoover suggested the source could be a man named Mort Halperin (a Kissinger staffer) and another man who worked in the Systems Analysis Agency. . . . According to Hoover's memo, Kissinger hoped "I would follow it up as far as we can take it and they will destroy whoever did this if we can find him, no matter where he is."
>
> The last line of that memo gives an accurate reflection of Henry's rage, as I remember it.
>
> Nevertheless, Nixon was one hundred percent behind the wiretaps. And

I was, too. And so the program started, inspired by Henry's rage but ordered by Nixon, who soon broadened it even further to include newsmen. Eventually, seventeen people were wiretapped by the FBI including seven on Kissinger's NSC staff and three on the White House staff.

And thus occurred the birth of the "plumbers" and of the assault on American law and democracy that they inaugurated. Commenting on the lamentable end of this process, Haldeman wrote that he still believed that ex-President Nixon (who was then still alive) should agree to the release of the remaining tapes. But:

> This time my view is apparently not shared by the man who was one reason for the original decision to start the taping process. Henry Kissinger is determined to stop the tapes from reaching the public. . . .
>
> Nixon made the point that Kissinger was really the one who had the most to lose from the tapes becoming public. Henry apparently felt that the tapes would expose a lot of things he had said that would be very disadvantageous to him publicly.
>
> Nixon said that in making the deal for custody of his Presidential papers, which was originally announced after his pardon but then was shot down by Congress, it was Henry who called him and insisted on Nixon's right to destroy the tapes. That was, of course, the thing that destroyed the deal.

A society that has been "plumbed" has the right to demand that its plumbers be compelled to make some restitution by way of full disclosure. The litigation to put the Nixon tapes in the public trust is only partially complete; no truthful account of the Vietnam years will be complete until Kissinger's part in what we already know has been made fully transparent.

Until that time, Kissinger's role in the violation of American law at the close of the Vietnam war makes the perfect counterpart to the 1968 covert action that helped him to power in the first place. The two parentheses enclose a series of premeditated war crimes which still have power to stun the imagination.

4

BANGLADESH: ONE GENOCIDE, ONE COUP AND ONE ASSASSINATION

THE ANNALS OF American diplomacy contain many imperishable pages of humanism, which may, and should, be set against some of the squalid and dispiriting traffic recorded in these pages. One might cite the extraordinary 1915 despatches of Ambassador Henry Morgenthau from his post in Ottoman Turkey, in which he employed consular and intelligence reports to give a picture of the deliberate state massacre of the Armenian minority, the first genocide of the twentieth century. (The word "genocide" having not then been coined, Ambassador Morgenthau had recourse to the – in some ways more expressive – term "race murder.")

By 1971, the word "genocide" was all too easily understood. It surfaced in a cable of protest from the United States consulate in what was then East Pakistan – the Bengali "wing" of the Muslim state of Pakistan, known to its restive nationalist inhabitants by the name Bangladesh. The cable was written on 6 April 1971 and its senior signatory, the Consul General in Dacca, was named Archer Blood. But it might have become known as the Blood Telegram in any case. Also sent directly to Washington, it differed from Morgenthau's document in one respect. It was not so much reporting on genocide as denouncing the complicity of the United States government in genocide. Its main section read thus:

Our government has failed to denounce the suppression of democracy. Our government has failed to denounce atrocities. Our government has failed to take forceful measures to protect its citizens while at the same time bending over backwards to placate the West Pak[istan] dominated government and to lessen any deservedly negative international public relations impact against them. Our government has evidenced what many will consider moral bankruptcy, ironically at a time when the USSR sent President Yahya Khan a message defending democracy, condemning the arrest of a leader of a democratically-elected majority party, incidentally pro-West, and calling for an end to repressive measures and bloodshed.... But we have chosen not to intervene, even morally, on the grounds that the Awami conflict, *in which unfortunately the overworked term genocide is applicable,* is purely an internal matter of a sovereign state. Private Americans have expressed disgust. We, as professional civil servants, express our dissent with current policy and fervently hope that our true and lasting interests here can be defined and our policies redirected.

This was signed by twenty members of the United States diplomatic team in Bangladesh and, on its arrival at the State Department, by a further nine senior officers in the South Asia division. It was the most public and the most strongly worded démarche from State Department servants to the State Department that has ever been recorded.

The circumstances fully warranted the protest. In December 1970, the Pakistani military elite had permitted the first open elections for a decade. The vote was easily won by Sheik Mujibur Rahman, the leader of the Bengali-based Awami League, who gained a large overall majority in the proposed National Assembly. (In the East alone, it won 167 out of 169 seats.) This, among other things, meant a challenge to the political and military and economic hegemony of the Western "wing." The National Assembly had been scheduled to meet on 3 March 1971. On 1 March, General Yahya Khan, head of the supposedly outgoing military regime, postponed its convening. This resulted in mass protests and nonviolent civil disobedience in the East.

On 25 March, the Pakistani army struck at the Bengali capital of Dacca. Having arrested and kidnapped Rahman, and taken him to West Pakistan, it set about massacring his supporters. The foreign press had been pre-emptively expelled from the city, but much of the direct evidence of what then happened was provided via a radio transmitter operated by the United States consulate. Archer Blood himself supplied an account of one episode directly to the State Department and to Henry Kissinger's National Security Council. Having readied the ambush, Pakistani regular soldiers set fire to the women's dormitory at the university, and then mowed the occupants down with machine guns as they sought to escape. (The guns, along with all the other weaponry, had been furnished under United States military assistance programs.)

Other reports, since amply vindicated, were supplied to the London *Times* and *Sunday Times* by the courageous reporter Anthony Mascarhenas, and flashed around a horrified world. Rape, murder, dismemberment and the state murder of children were employed as deliberate methods of repression and intimidation. At least ten thousand civilians were butchered in the first three days. The eventual civilian death toll has never been placed at less than half a million and has been put as high as three million. Since almost all Hindu citizens were at risk by definition from Pakistani military chauvinism (not that Pakistan's Muslim co-religionists were spared), a vast movement of millions of refugees – perhaps as many as ten million – began to cross the Indian frontier. To summarize, then: first, the direct negation of a democratic election; second, the unleashing of a genocidal policy; third, the creation of a very dangerous international crisis. Within a short time, Ambassador Kenneth Keating, the ranking United States diplomat in New Delhi, had added his voice to those of the dissenters. It was a time, he told Washington, when a principled stand against the authors of this aggression and atrocity would also make the best pragmatic sense. Keating, a former senator from New York, used a very suggestive phrase in his cable of 29 March 1971, calling on the administration to "promptly, publicly, and prominently deplore this brutality." It was "most important these actions be taken now," he warned, "prior to inevitable and imminent emergence of horrible truths."

Nixon and Kissinger acted quickly. That is to say, Archer Blood was immediately recalled from his post, and Ambassador Keating was described by the President to Kissinger, with some contempt, as having been "taken over by the Indians." In late April 1971, at the very height of the mass murder, Kissinger sent a message to General Yahya Khan, thanking him for his "delicacy and tact."

We now know of one reason why the general was so favored, at a time when he had made himself – and his patrons – responsible for the grossest war crimes and crimes against humanity. In April 1971, a United States ping-pong team had accepted a surprise invitation to compete in Beijing and by the end of that month, using the Pakistani ambassador as an intermediary, the Chinese authorities had forwarded a letter inviting Nixon to send an envoy. Thus there was one motive of realpolitik for the shame that Nixon and Kissinger were to visit on their own country for its complicity in the extermination of the Bengalis.

Those who like to plead realpolitik, however, might wish to consider some further circumstances. There already was, and had been for some time, a back channel between Washington and Beijing. It ran through Nicolae Ceausescu's Romania – not a much more decorative choice but not, at that stage, a positively criminal one. There was no reason to confine approaches, to a serious person like Chou En Lai, to the narrow channel afforded by a blood-soaked (and short-lived, as it turned out) despot like the "delicate and tactful" Yahya Khan. Either Chou En Lai wanted contact, in other words, or he did not. As Lawrence Lifschultz, the primary historian of this period, has put it:

> Winston Lord, Kissinger's deputy at the National Security Council, stressed to investigators the internal rationalisation developed within the upper echelons of the Administration. Lord told [the staff of the Carnegie Endowment for International Peace] "We had to demonstrate to China we were a reliable government to deal with. We had to show China that we respect a mutual friend." How, after two decades of belligerent animosity with the People's Republic, mere support for Pakistan in its bloody civil war was supposed to

demonstrate to China that the US "was a reliable government to deal with" was a mystifying proposition which more cynical observers of the events, both in and outside the US government, consider to have been an excuse justifying the simple convenience of the Islamabad link – a link which Washington had no overriding desire to shift.

Second, the knowledge of this secret diplomacy and its accompanying privileges obviously freed the Pakistani general of such restraints as might have inhibited him. He told his closest associates, including his minister of information, G.W. Choudhury, that his private understanding with Washington and Beijing would protect him. Choudhury later wrote: "If Nixon and Kissinger had not given him that false hope, he'd have been more realistic." Thus, the collusion with him in the matter of China *increases* the direct complicity of Nixon and Kissinger in the massacres. (There is another consideration outside the scope of this book, which involves the question: why did Kissinger confine his China diplomacy to channels provided by authoritarian or totalitarian regimes? Why was an open diplomacy not just as easy, if not easier? The answer – which also lies outside the scope of this book – is apparently that surreptitiousness, while not essential in itself, was essential if Nixon and Kissinger were going to be able to take the credit for it.)

It cannot possibly be argued, in any case, that the saving of Kissinger's private correspondence with China was worth the deliberate sacrifice of hundreds of thousands of Bengali civilians. And – which is worse still – later and fuller disclosures now allow us to doubt that this was indeed the whole motive. The Kissinger policy towards Bangladesh may well have been largely conducted for its own sake, as a means of gratifying his boss's animus against India and as a means of preventing the emergence of Bangladesh as a self-determining state in any case.

The diplomatic commonplace term "tilt" – signifying that mixture of signals and nuances and codes that describe a foreign policy preference that is often too embarrassing to be openly avowed – actually originates in this dire episode. On 6 March 1971, Kissinger summoned a meeting at the

National Security Council and – *in advance of* the crisis in East–West Pakistan relations that was by then palpable and predictable to those attending – insisted that no preemptive action be taken. Those present who suggested that a warning to General Yahya Khan be issued, essentially advising him to honor the election results, he strongly opposed. His subsequent policy was as noted above. After returning from China in July, he began to speak in almost Maoist phrases about a Soviet–Indian plot to dismember and even annex part of Pakistan, which would compel China to intervene on Pakistan's side. (In pursuit of this fantasy of confrontation, he annoyed Admiral Elmo Zumwalt by ordering him to despatch the aircraft carrier USS *Enterprise* from the coast of Vietnam to the Bay of Bengal, while giving it no stated mission.) But no analyst in the State Department or the CIA could be found to underwrite such a bizarre prediction and, at a meeting of the Senior Review Group, Kissinger lost his temper with this insubordination. "The President always says to tilt toward Pakistan, but every proposal I get is in the opposite direction. Sometimes I think I'm in a nuthouse." The Nixon White House was, as it happens, in the process of becoming exactly that, but his hearers only had time to notice that a new power-term had entered Washington's vernacular of crisis and conspiracy.

"The President always says to tilt toward Pakistan." That at least was true. Long before any conception of his "China diplomacy," indeed even during the years when he was inveighing against "Red China" and its sympathizers, Nixon detested the government of India and expressed warm sympathy for Pakistan. Many of his biographers and intimates, including Kissinger, have recorded the particular dislike he felt (more justifiably, perhaps) for the person of Indira Gandhi. He always referred to her as "that bitch" and on one occasion kept her waiting for an unprecedented forty-five minutes outside his White House door. However, the dislike originated with Nixon's loathing for her father Pandit Nehru, and with his more general loathing for Nehru's sponsorship – along with Makarios, Tito and Soekarno – of the Non-Aligned Movement. There can be no doubt that, with or without an occluded "China card," General Yahya Khan would have enjoyed a sympathic hearing, and treatment, from this president, and thus from this national security advisor.

This is also strongly suggested by Kissinger's subsequent conduct, as Secretary of State, towards Bangladesh as a country and towards Sheik Mujib, leader of the Awami League and later the father of Bangladeshi independence, as a politician. Unremitting hostility and contempt were the signature elements in both cases. Kissinger had received some very bad and even mocking press for his handling of the Bangladesh crisis, and it had somewhat spoiled his supposedly finest hour in China. He came to resent the Bangladeshis and their leader, and even compared (this according to his then aide Roger Morris) Mujib to Allende.

As soon as Kissinger became Secretary of State in 1973, he downgraded all those who had signed the genocide protest in 1971. In the fall of the next year, 1974, he inflicted a series of snubs on Mujib, then on his first visit to the United States as head of state. In Washington Kissinger boycotted the fifteen-minute meeting that Mujib was allowed by President Ford. He also opposed Mujib's main request, which was for emergency United States grain shipments, and some help with debt relief, in order to recuperate the country so ravaged by Kissinger's friend and ally. To cite Roger Morris again: "In Kissinger's view there was very much a distant hands-off attitude toward them. Since they had the audacity to become independent of one of my client states, they will damn well float on their own for a while." It was at about this time that Kissinger was heard to pronounce Bangladesh "an international basket case," a judgment which, to the extent that it was true, was also self-fulfilling.

In November 1974, on a brief face-saving tour of the region, Kissinger made an eight-hour stop in Bangladesh and gave a three-minute press conference in which he refused to say why he had sent the USS *Enterprise* into the Bay of Bengal three years before. Within a few weeks of his departure, we now know, a faction at the US embassy in Dacca began covertly meeting with a group of Bangladeshi officers who were planning a coup against Mujib. On 14 August 1975, Mujib and forty members of his family were murdered in a military takeover. His closest former political associates were bayoneted to death in their prison cells a few months after that.[*]

The Senate Foreign Relations Committee was at that time conducting its sensational inquiries into CIA involvement with assassinations and subversion in the Third World. The "two track" concept, whereby an American ambassador like Ed Korry in Chile could find that his intelligence officers and military attachés were going behind his back and over his head, with secret authorizations from Washington, and running their own show, had not become a familiar one. However, exhaustive research by Lawrence Lifschultz of Yale University now strongly suggests that a "two track" scheme was implemented in Bangladesh as well.

The man installed as Bangladesh's president by the young officers who had slain Rahman was Khondakar Mustaque, generally identified as the leader of the right-wing element within the Awami League. He was at pains to say that the coup had come to him as a complete surprise, and that the young majors who had led it – Major Farooq, Major Rashid and four others, at the head of a detachment numbering just three hundred men – had "acted on their own." He added that he had never met the mutinous officers before. Such denials are of course customary, almost matters of etiquette. So are the ensuing statements from Washington, which invariably claim that this or that political upheaval has taken the world's largest and most powerful intelligence-gathering system completely off guard. That expected statement, too, was made in the aftermath of the assassination in Dacca.

The cover story (one might term it the coincidence version) leaks at every joint and comes apart at the most cursory inspection. Major Rashid was interviewed by Anthony Mascarhenas, the journalistic hero of the

---

[*] In December 2000 those responsible were convicted by a Bangladeshi court and (wrongly, in my opinion) sentenced to death. Some of the accused were unavailable for sentencing because they had taken refuge in the United States: a feat not achievable by the average Bengali immigrant.

Bangladesh war, on the anniversary of the coup. He confirmed that he had met Mustaque before the coup, and again on the days immediately preceding it. In fact, a senior Bangladeshi officer has dated meetings between Mustaque and the mutineers more than six months before Mujib's overthrow.

The United States ambassador in Dacca, Davis Eugene Booster, was aware that a coup was being discussed. He was also aware of the highly controversial congressional hearings in Washington, which had unveiled high-level official wrongdoing and ruined the career of many a careless foreign service officer. He ordered that all contact between his embassy and the mutinous officers be terminated. Thus his alarm and annoyance, on 14 August 1975, was great. The men who had seized power were the very ones with whom he had ordered a cessation of contact. Embassy sources have since confirmed to Lifschultz (a) that United States officials had been approached by, and had by no means discouraged, the officers who intended a coup and (b) that Ambassador Booster became convinced that his CIA station was operating a back channel without his knowledge. Such an operation would be meaningless, and also pointlessly risky, if it did not extend homeward to Washington where, as is now notorious, the threads of the Forty Committee and the National Security Council were very closely held in one fist.

Philip Cherry, the then head of the CIA station in Bangladesh, was interviewed by Lifschultz in September 1978. He was vague and evasive even about having held the job but did say, "There is one thing. There are politicians who frequently approach embassies, and perhaps have contacts there. They think they may have contacts." The shift from officer to politician is suggestive. And, of course, those who think they may have contacts may even act as if they do, unless they are otherwise advised.

Not only did Khondakar Mustaque *think* he had contacts with the United States government, including with Henry Kissinger himself, but he did indeed have such contacts, and had had since 1971. In 1973 in Washington, and in the aftermath of the unprecedented revolt of professional diplomats against the Kissinger policy in Bangladesh, the Carnegie

Endowment for International Peace (publisher of the magazine *Foreign Policy*) conducted a full-dress study of the "tilt" that had put the United States on the same side as those committing genocide. More than 150 senior officials from the State Department and the CIA agreed to be interviewed. The study was coordinated by Kissinger's former aide Roger Morris. The result of the nine-month inquiry was never made public, due to internal differences at Carnegie, but the material was made available to Lifschultz and it does establish one conclusion beyond doubt.

In 1971 Henry Kissinger had attempted the impossible by trying to divide the electorally victorious Awami League, and to dilute its demand for independence. In pursuit of this favor to General Yahya Khan, he had initiated a covert approach to Khondakar Mustaque, who led the tiny minority who were willing to compromise on the main principle. A recently unearthed "Memorandum for the Record" gives us details of a White House meeting between Nixon, Kissinger and others on 11 August 1971, at which Undersecretary of State John Irwin reported: "We have had reports in recent days of the possibility that some Awami League leaders in Calcutta want to negotiate with Yahya on the basis of giving up their claim for the independence of East Pakistan." This can only have been a reference to the Provisional Government of Bangladesh, set up in exile in Calcutta after the massacres, and could only have been an attempt to circumvent its leadership. The consequences of this clumsy approach were that Mustaque was exposed and placed under house arrest in October 1971, and that the American political officer who contacted him, George Griffin, was declared *persona non grata* when gazetted to the US embassy in New Delhi a decade later.

Those involved in the military preparations for the coup have told Lifschultz that they, too, had a "two track" policy. There were junior officers ready to mutiny and there was a senior officer – the future dictator General Zia – who was ready but more hesitant. Both factions say that they naturally checked with their United States contacts in advance, and were told that the overthrow of Mujib was "no problem." This is at least partially confirmed by a signed letter from Congressman Stephen J. Solarz of the House Foreign Affairs Committee, who undertook to investigate the matter for Lifschultz in 1980 and who on 3 June of that year wrote to him: "With respect to the Embassy meetings in the November 1974–January 1975 period with opponents of the Rahman regime, the State Department once again does not deny that the meetings took place." This would appear to be a rebuff to the evidence of Mr Cherry of the CIA, even if the letter goes on to say: "The Department does claim that it notified Rahman about the meetings, including the possibility of a coup." If true, that "claim" is being made for the first time, and in the name of the man who was murdered during the coup and cannot refute it. The admission is stronger than the claim in any case.

Congressman Solarz forwarded the questions about CIA involvement to the office of Congressman Les Aspin of the Permanent Select Committee on Intelligence, which committee, as he said, "has the best chance of obtaining access both to CIA cable traffic and to the relevant figures in the intelligence community." But the letter he sent was somehow lost along the way, and was never received by the relevant inquiring committee, and shortly afterwards the balance of power in Washington shifted from Carter to Reagan.

Only a reopened congressional inquiry with subpoena power could determine whether there was any direct connection, apart from the self-evident ones of consistent statecraft attested by recurring reliable testimony, between the secret genocidal diplomacy of 1971 and the secret destabilizing diplomacy of 1975. The task of disproving such a connection, meanwhile, would appear to rest on those who believe that everything is an accident.

5

CHILE

IN A FAMOUS expression of his contempt for democracy, Kissinger once observed that he saw no reason why a certain country should be allowed to "go Marxist" merely because "its people are irresponsible." The country concerned was Chile, which at the time of this remark had a justified reputation as the most highly evolved pluralistic democracy in the southern hemisphere of the Americas. The pluralism translated, in the years of the Cold War, into an electorate that voted about one-third conservative, one-third socialist and communist, and one-third Christian Democratic and centrist. This had made it relatively easy to keep the Marxist element from having its turn in government, and ever since 1962 the CIA had – as it had in Italy and other comparable nations – largely contented itself with funding the reliable elements. In September 1970, however, the Left's candidate actually gained a slight plurality of 36.2 percent in the presidential elections. Divisions on the Right, and the adherence of some smaller radical and Christian parties to the Left, made it a moral certainty that the Chilean Congress would, after the traditional sixty-day interregnum, confirm Dr Salvador Allende as the next president. But the very name of Allende was anathema to the extreme Right in Chile, to certain powerful corporations (notably ITT, Pepsi Cola and the Chase Manhattan Bank) which did business in Chile and the United States, and to the CIA.

This loathing quickly communicated itself to President Nixon. He was personally beholden to Donald Kendall, the President of Pepsi Cola, who had given him his first corporate account when, as a young lawyer, he had joined John Mitchell's New York firm. A series of Washington meetings, held within eleven days of Allende's electoral victory, essentially settled the fate of Chilean democracy. After discussions with Kendall and with David Rockefeller of Chase Manhattan, and with CIA director Richard Helms, Kissinger went with Helms to the Oval Office. Helms's notes of the meeting show that Nixon wasted little breath in making his wishes known. Allende was not to assume office. "Not concerned risks involved. No involvement of embassy. $10,000,000 available, more if necessary. Full-time job – best men we have. . . . Make the economy scream. 48 hours for plan of action."

Declassified documents show that Kissinger – who had previously neither known nor cared about Chile, describing it offhandedly as "a dagger pointed at the heart of Antarctica" – took seriously this chance to impress his boss. A group was set up in Langley, Virginia, with the express purpose of running a "two track" policy for Chile: one the ostensible diplomatic one and the other – unknown to the State Department or the US ambassador to Chile, Edward Korry – a strategy of destabilization, kidnap and assassination, designed to provoke a military coup.

There were long- and short-term obstacles to the incubation of such an intervention, especially in the brief interval available before Allende took his oath of office. The long-term obstacle was the tradition of military abstention from politics in Chile, a tradition which marked off the country from its neighbors. Such a military culture was not to be degraded overnight. The short-term obstacle lay in the person of one man – General René Schneider. As chief of the Chilean General Staff, he was adamantly opposed to any military meddling in the electoral process. Accordingly, it was decided at a meeting on 18 September 1970 that General Schneider had to go.

The plan was to have him kidnapped by extremist officers, in such a way as to make it appear that leftist and pro-Allende elements were behind the plot. The resulting confusion, it was hoped, would panic the Chilean Congress into denying Allende the presidency. A sum of $50,000 was offered around the Chilean capital, Santiago, for any officer or officers enterprising enough to take on this task. Richard Helms and his director of covert operations, Thomas Karamessines, told Kissinger that they were not optimistic. Military circles were hesitant and divided, or else loyal to General Schneider and the Chilean constitution. As Helms put it in a later account of the conversation, "We tried to make clear to Kissinger how small the possibility of success was." Kissinger firmly told Helms and Karamessines to press on in any case.

Here one must pause for a recapitulation. An unelected official in the United States is meeting with others, without the knowledge or authorization of Congress, to plan the kidnapping of a constitution-minded senior officer in a democratic country with which the United States is not at war, and with which it maintains cordial diplomatic relations. The minutes of the meetings may have an official look to them (though they were hidden from the light of day for long enough) but what we are reviewing is a "hit" – a piece of state-supported terrorism.

Ambassador Korry has testified that he told his embassy staff to have nothing to do with a group styling itself *Patria y Libertad* (Fatherland and Freedom), a quasi-fascist group intent on defying the election results. He sent three cables to Washington warning his superiors to have nothing to do with them either. He was unaware that his own military attachés had been told to contact the group and keep the fact from him. And when the outgoing president of Chile, the Christian Democrat Eduardo Frei, announced that he was opposed to any US intervention and would vote to confirm the legally elected Allende, it was precisely to this gang that Kissinger turned. On 15 October 1970, Kissinger was told of an extremist right-wing officer named General Roberto Viaux, who had ties to *Patria y Libertad* and who was willing to accept the secret US commission to remove General Schneider from the chessboard. The term "kidnap" was still being employed at this point, and is often employed still. However, Kissinger's Track Two group authorized the supply of machine guns as well as tear gas grenades to Viaux's associates, and never seems to have asked what they would do with the general once they had kidnapped him.

Let the documents tell the story. A CIA cable to Kissinger's Track Two group from Santiago dated 18 October 1970 reads (with the names still blacked out for "security" purposes and cover identities written in by hand – in my square brackets – by the ever-thoughtful redaction service):

1. [Station cooptee] met clandestinely evening 17 Oct with [two Chilean armed forces officers] who told him their plans were moving along better than had thought possible. They asked that by evening 18 Oct [cooptee] arrange furnish them with eight to ten tear gas grenades. Within 48 hours they need three 45 calibre machine guns ("grease guns") with 500 rounds ammo each. [One officer] commented has three machine guns himself but can be identified by serial numbers as having been issued to him therefore unable use them.

2. [Officers] said they have to move because they believe they now under suspicion and being watched by Allende supporters. [One officer] was late to meeting having taken evasive action to shake possible surveillance by one or two taxi cabs with dual antennas which he believed being used by opposition against him.

3. [Cooptee] asked if [officers] had Air Force contacts. They answered they did not but would welcome one. [Cooptee] separately has since tried contact [a Chilean Air Force General] and will keep trying until established. Will urge [Air Force General] meet with [other two officers] a.s.a.p. [Cooptee] commented to station that [Air Force General] has not tried contact him since ref a talk.

4. [Cooptee] comment: cannot tell who is leader of this movement but strongly suspects it is Admiral [Deleted]. It would appear from [his contact's] actions and alleged Allende suspicions about them that unless they act now they are lost. Trying get more info from them evening 18 Oct about support they believe they have.

5. Station plans give six tear gas grenades (arriving noon 18 Oct by special courier) to [cooptee] for delivery to [armed forces officers] instead of having [false flag officer] deliver them to Viaux group. Our reasoning is that

[cooptee] dealing with active duty officers. Also [false flag officer] leaving evening 18 Oct and will not be replaced but [cooptee] will stay here. Hence important that [cooptee] credibility with [armed forces officers] be strengthened by prompt delivery what they requesting. Request headquarters agreement by 1500 hours local time 18 Oct on decision delivery of tear gas to [cooptee] vice [false flag officer].

6. Request prompt shipment three sterile 45 calibre machine guns and ammo per para 1 above, by special courier if necessary. Please confirm by 2000 hours local time 18 Oct that this can be done so [cooptee] may inform his contacts accordingly.

The reply, which is headed "IMMEDIATE SANTIAGO (EYES ONLY [DELETED])" is dated 18 October and reads:

Sub-machine guns and ammo being sent by regular [deleted] courier leaving Washington 0700 hours 19 October due arrive Santiago late evening 20 October or early morning 21 October. Preferred use regular [deleted] courier to avoid bringing undue attention to op.

A companion message, also addressed to "Santiago 562," went like this:

1. Depending how [cooptee] conversation goes evening 18 October you may wish submit Intel report [deleted] so we can decide whether should be dissemed.

2. New subject. If [cooptee] plans lead coup, or be actively and publicly involved, we puzzled why it should bother him if machine guns can be traced to him. Can we develop rationale on why guns must be sterile? Will continue make effort provide them but find our credulity stretched by Navy [officer] leading his troops with sterile guns? What is special purpose for these guns? We will try send them whether you can provide explanation or not.

The full beauty of this cable traffic cannot be appreciated without a reading of another message, dated 16 October. (It must be borne in mind that the Chilean Congress was to meet to confirm Allende as president on the 24th of that month.)

1. [Deleted/handwritten code name Trickturn] policy, objectives and actions were reviewed at high USG [United States Government] level afternoon 15 October. Conclusions, which are to be your operational guide, follow:

2. It is firm and continuing policy that Allende be overthrown by a coup. It would be much preferable to have this transpire prior to 24 October but efforts in this regard will continue vigorously beyond this date. We are to continue to generate maximum pressure toward this end utilizing every appropriate resource. *It is imperative that these actions be implemented clandestinely and securely so that the USG and American hand be well hidden.* [italics added] While this imposes on us a high degree of selectivity in making military contacts and dictates that these contacts be made in the most secure manner it definitely does not preclude contacts such as reported in Santiago 544 which was a masterful piece of work.

3. After the most careful consideration it was determined that a Viaux coup attempt carried out by him alone with the forces now at his disposal would fail. Thus, it would be counterproductive to our [deleted; handwritten insert "Track Two"] objectives. It was decided that [deleted; handwritten insert "CIA"] get a message to Viaux warning him against precipitate action. In essence our message is to state, "We have reviewed your plans, and based on your information and ours, we come to the conclusion that your plans for a coup at this time cannot succeed. Failing, they may reduce your capabilities for the future. Preserve your assets. We will stay in touch. The time will come when you together with all your other friends can do something. You will continue to have our support." You are requested to deliver the message to Viaux essentially as noted above. Our objectives are as follows: (A) To advise him of our opinion and discourage him from acting alone; (B) Continue to encourage him to amplify his planning; (C) Encourage him to join forces with other coup planners so that they may act in concert either before or after 24 October. (N.B. Six gas masks and six CS cannisters [*sic*] are being carried to Santiago by special [deleted] courier ETD Washington 1100 hours 16 October.)

4. There is great and continuing interest in the activities of Tirado, Canales, Valenzuela et al and we wish them maximum good fortune.

5. The above is your operating guidance. No other policy guidance you may receive from [indecipherable: State?] or its maximum exponent in Santiago, on his return, are to sway you from your course.

6. Please review all your present and possibly new activities to include prop-aganda, black operations, surfacing of intelligence or disinformation, personal contacts, or anything else your imagination can conjure which will permit you to press forward our [deleted] objective in a secure manner.

Finally, it is essential to read the White House "memorandum of conversa-tion," dated 15 October 1970, to which the above cable directly refers and of which it is a more honest summary. Present for the "high USG level" meet-ing were, as noted in the heading: "Dr Kissinger, Mr Karamessines, Gen. Haig." The first paragraph of their deliberations has been entirely blacked out, with not so much as a scribble in the margin from the redaction serv-ice. (Given what has since been admitted, this twenty-line deletion must be well worth reading.) Picking up at paragraph two, we find the following:

2. Then Mr Karamessines provided a run-down on Viaux, the Canales meet-ing with Tirado, the latter's new position [after Porta was relieved of command "for health reasons"] and, in some detail, the general situation in Chile from the coup possibility viewpoint.

3. A certain amount of information was available to us concerning Viaux's alleged support throughout the Chilean military. We had assessed Viaux's claims carefully, basing our analysis on good intelligence from a number of sources. Our conclusion was clear: Viaux did not have more than one chance in twenty – perhaps less – to launch a successful coup.

4. The unfortunate repercussions, in Chile and internationally, of an unsuc-cessful coup were discussed. Dr Kissinger ticked off his list of these negative possibilities. His items were remarkably similar to the ones Mr Karamessines had prepared.

5. It was decided by those present that the Agency must get a message to Viaux warning him against any precipitate action. In essence our message was to state: "We have reviewed your plans, and based on your information and ours, we come to the conclusion that your plans for a coup at this time cannot succeed. Failing, they may reduce your capabilities for the future. Preserve your assets. We will stay in touch. The time will come when you with all your other friends can do something. You will continue to have our support."

6. After the decision to de-fuse the Viaux coup plot, *at least temporarily*, Dr Kissinger instructed Mr Karamessines to preserve Agency assets in Chile, working clandestinely and securely to maintain the capability for Agency operations against Allende in the future.

7. Dr Kissinger discussed his desire that the word of our encouragement to the Chilean military in recent weeks be kept as secret as possible. Mr Karamessines stated emphatically that we had been doing everything possible in this connection, including the use of false flag officers, car meetings and every conceivable precaution. But we and others had done a great deal of talking recently with a number of persons. For example, Ambassador Korry's wideranging discussions with numerous people urging a coup "cannot be put back into the bottle." [Three lines of deletion follow.] [Dr Kissinger requested that copy of the message be sent to him on 16 October.]

8. The meeting concluded on Dr Kissinger's note that the Agency should continue keeping the pressure on every Allende weak spot in sight: – now, after the 24th of October, after 5 November, and into the future until such time as new marching orders are given. Mr Karamessines stated that the Agency would comply.

So Track Two contained two tracks of its own. Track Two/One was the group of ultras led by General Roberto Viaux and his sidekick Captain Arturo Marshal. These men had tried to bring off a coup in 1969 against the Christian Democrats; they had been cashiered and were disliked even by conservatives in the officer corps. "Track Two/Two" was a more ostensibly "respectable" faction headed by General Camilo Valenzuela, the chief of the garrison in the capital city, whose name occurs in the cables above and whose identity is concealed by some of the deletions. Several of the CIA operatives in Chile felt that Viaux was too much of a mad-dog to be trusted. And Ambassador Korry's repeated admonitions also had their effect. As shown in the 15 October memo cited above, Kissinger and Karamessines developed last-minute second thoughts about Viaux, who as late as 13 October had been given $20,000 in cash from the CIA station and promised a life insurance policy of $250,000. This offer was authorized direct from the White House. However, with only days to go before Allende was inaugurated, and with Nixon repeating that "it was absolutely essential that the election of Mr Allende to the Presidency be thwarted," the pressure on the Valenzuela group became intense. As a direct consequence, especially after the warm words of encouragement he had been given, General Roberto Viaux felt himself under some obligation to deliver also, and to disprove those who had doubted him.

On the evening of 19 October 1970, the Valenzuela group, aided by some of Viaux's gang, and equipped with the tear gas grenades delivered by the CIA, attempted to grab General Schneider as he left an official dinner. The attempt failed because he left in a private car and not the expected official vehicle. The failure produced an extremely significant cable from CIA headquarters in Washington to the local station, asking for urgent action because "Headquarters must respond during morning 20 October to queries from high levels." Payments of $50,000 each to General Viaux and his chief associate were then authorized on condition that they made another attempt. On the evening of 20 October, they did. But again there was only failure to report. On 22 October, the "sterile" machine guns above-mentioned were handed to Valenzuela's group for another try. Later that same day, General Roberto Viaux's gang finally murdered General René Schneider.

According to the later verdict of the Chilean military courts, this atrocity partook of elements of both tracks of Track Two. In other words, Valenzuela was not himself on the scene but the assassination squad, led by Viaux, contained men who had participated in the preceding two attempts. Viaux was convicted on charges of kidnapping and of conspiring to cause a coup. Valenzuela was convicted of the charge of conspiracy to cause a coup. So any subsequent attempt to distinguish the two plots from each other, except in point of degree, is an attempt to confect a distinction without a difference.

It scarcely matters whether Schneider was slain because of a kidnapping scheme that went awry (he was said, but only by the assassins, to have had the temerity to resist) or whether his assassination was the objective in the first place. The Chilean military police report, as it happens, describes a straightforward murder. Under the law of every law-bound country (including the United States), a crime committed in the pursuit of a kidnapping is thereby aggravated, not mitigated. You may not say, with a corpse at your feet, "I was only trying to kidnap him." At least, you may not say so if you hope to plead extenuating circumstances.

Yet a version of "extenuating circumstances" has become the paper-thin cover story with which Kissinger has since protected himself from the charge of being an accomplice, before and after the fact, in kidnap and murder. And this sorry cover story has even found a refuge in the written record. The Senate Intelligence Committee, in its investigation of the matter, concluded that since the machine guns supplied to Valenzuela had not actually been employed in the killing, and since General Viaux had been officially discouraged by the CIA a few days before the murder, there was therefore "no evidence of a plan to kill Schneider or that United States officials specifically anticipated that Schneider would be shot during the abduction."

Walter Isaacson, one of Kissinger's biographers, takes at face value a memo from Kissinger to Nixon after his meeting on 15 October with Karamessines, in which he reports to the President that he had "turned off" the Viaux plot. He also takes at face value the claim that Viaux's successful hit was essentially unauthorized.

These excuses and apologies are as logically feeble as they are morally contemptible. Henry Kissinger bears direct responsibility for the Schneider murder, as the following points demonstrate.

1. Brian MacMaster, one of the "false flag" agents mentioned in the cable traffic above, a career CIA man carrying a forged Colombian passport and claiming to represent American business interests in Chile, has told of his efforts to get "hush money" to jailed members of the Viaux group, *after* the assassination and before they could implicate the Agency.

2. Colonel Paul M. Wimert, a military attaché in Santiago and chief

CIA liaison with the Valenzuela faction, has testified that after the Schneider killing he hastily retrieved the two payments of $50,000 that had been paid to Valenzuela and his partner, and also the three "sterile" machine guns. He then drove rapidly to the Chilean seaside town of Vina del Mar and hurled the guns into the ocean. His accomplice in this action, CIA station chief Henry Hecksher, had assured Washington only days before that *either* Viaux *or* Valenzuela would be able to eliminate Schneider and thereby trigger a coup.

3. Look again at the White House/Kissinger memo of 15 October, and at the doggedly literal way it is retransmitted to Chile. In no sense of the term does it "turn off" Viaux. If anything, it incites him – a well-known and boastful fanatic – to redouble his efforts. "Preserve your assets. We will stay in touch. The time will come when you together with all your other friends can do something.You will continue to have our support." This is not exactly the language of standing him down. The remainder of the memo speaks plainly of the intention to "discourage him from acting *alone*," to "continue to *encourage* him to amplify his planning" and to "*encourage* him to join forces with other coup planners so that they may act in concert either before or after 24 October" (italics added). The last three stipulations are an entirely accurate, not to say prescient, description of what Viaux actually did.

4. Consult again the cable received by Henry Hecksher on 20 October, referring to anxious queries "from high levels" about the first of the failed attacks on Schneider. Thomas Karamessines, when questioned by the Senate Intelligence Committee about this cable, testified of his certainty that the words "high levels" referred directly to Kissinger. In all previous communications from Washington, as a glance above will show, that had indeed been the case. This on its own is enough to demolish Kissinger's claim to have "turned off" Track Two (and its interior tracks) on 15 October.

5. Ambassador Korry later made the obvious point that Kissinger was attempting to build a paper alibi in the event of a failure by the Viaux

group. "His interest was not in Chile but in who was going to be blamed for what. He wanted me to be the one who took the heat. Henry didn't want to be associated with a failure and he was setting up a record to blame the State Department. He brought me in to the President because he wanted me to say what I had to say about Viaux; he wanted me to be the soft man."

The concept of "deniability" was not as well understood in Washington in 1970 as it has since become. But it is clear that Henry Kissinger wanted two things simultaneously. He wanted the removal of General Schneider, by any means and employing any proxy. (No instruction from Washington to leave Schneider unharmed was ever given; deadly weapons were sent by diplomatic pouch, and men of violence were carefully selected to receive them.) And he wanted to be out of the picture in case such an attempt might fail, or be uncovered. These are the normal motives of anyone who solicits or suborns murder. However, Kissinger needed the crime very slightly more than he needed, or was able to design, the deniability. Without waiting for his many hidden papers to be released or subpoenaed, we can say with safety that he is *prima facie* guilty of direct collusion in the murder of a democratic officer in a democratic and peaceful country.

There is no particular need to rehearse the continuing role of the Nixon–Kissinger administration in the later economic and political subversion and destabilization of the Allende government, and in the creation of favorable conditions for the military coup that occurred on 11 September 1973. Kissinger himself was perhaps no more and no less involved in this effort than any other high official in Nixon's national-security orbit. On 9 November 1970 he authored the National Security Council's "Decision Memorandum 93," reviewing policy towards Chile in the immediate wake of Allende's confirmation as President. Various routine measures of economic harassment were proposed (recall Nixon's instruction to "make the economy scream") with cutoffs in aid and investment.

More significantly, Kissinger advocated that "close relations" be maintained with military leaders in neighboring countries, in order to facilitate both the coordination of pressure against Chile and the incubation of opposition within the country. In outline, this prefigures the disclosures that have since been made about Operation Condor, a secret collusion between military dictatorships across the hemisphere, operated with United States knowledge and indulgence.

The actual overthrow of the Allende government in a bloody *coup d'état* took place while Kissinger was going through his own Senate confirmation process as Secretary of State. He falsely assured the Foreign Relations Committee that the United States government had played no part in the coup. From a thesaurus of hard information to the contrary, one might select Situation Report #2, from the Navy Section of the United States Military Group in Chile, and written by the US Naval Attaché, Patrick Ryan. Ryan describes his close relationship with the officers engaged in overthrowing the government, hails 11 September 1973 as "our D-Day" and observes with satisfaction that "Chile's coup de etat [*sic*] was close to perfect." Or one may peruse the declassified files on Project FUBELT – the code name under which the CIA, in frequent contact with Kissinger and the Forty Committee, conducted covert operations against the legal and elected government of Chile.

What is striking, and what points to a much more direct complicity in individual crimes against humanity, is the microcosmic detail in which Kissinger kept himself informed of Pinochet's atrocities.

On 16 November, Assistant Secretary of State Jack B. Kubisch delivered a detailed report on the Chilean junta's execution policy which, as he notes to the new secretary of state, "you requested by cable from Tokyo." The memo goes on to enlighten Kissinger in various ways about the first nineteen days of Pinochet's rule. Summary executions during that period, we are told, total 320. (This contrasts with the publicly announced total of 100, and is based on "an internal, confidential report prepared for the junta" to which US officials are evidently privy.) Looking on the bright side, "On

November 14, we announced our second CCC credit to Chile – $24 million for feed corn. Our longstanding commitment to sell two surplus destroyers to the Chilean navy has met a reasonably sympathetic response in Senate consultations. The Chileans, meanwhile, have sent us several new requests for controversial military equipment." Kubisch then raises the awkward question of two US citizens murdered by the junta – Frank Teruggi and Charles Horman – details of whose precise fate are still, more than a quarter-century later, being sought by their families. The reason for the length of the search may be inferred from a later comment by Mr Kubisch, dated 11 February 1974, in which he reports on a meeting with the junta's foreign minister, and notes that he raises the matter of the missing Americans "in the context of the need to be careful to keep relatively small issues in our relationship from making our cooperation more difficult."

To return, via this detour, to Operation Condor. This was a machinery of cross-border assassination, abduction, torture and intimidation, coordinated between the secret police forces of Pinochet's Chile, Stroessner's Paraguay, Videla's Argentina and other regional *caudillos*. This internationalization of the death-squad principle is now known to have been responsible, to name only the most salient victims, for the murder of the dissident general Carlos Prats of Chile (and his wife) in Buenos Aires, the murder of the Bolivian general Juan Jose Torres, and the maiming of a Chilean Christian Democrat senator, Bernardo Leighton, in Italy. A Condor team also detonated a car bomb in downtown Washington, DC, in September 1976, killing the former Chilean foreign minister Orlando Letelier and his aide Ronni Moffitt. United States government complicity has been uncovered at every level of this network. It has been established, for example, that the FBI aided Pinochet in capturing Jorge Isaac Fuentes de Alarcon, who was detained and tortured in Paraguay, then turned over to the Chilean secret police, and "disappeared." Astonishingly, the surveillance of Latin US dissident refugees in the United States was promised to Condor figures by US intelligence.

These and other facts have been established by the work of "truth and reconciliation" commissions set up by post-dictatorship forces in the countries of the southern hemisphere. Stroessner has been overthrown, Videla is in prison, Pinochet and his henchmen are being or have been brought to account in Chile. The United States has not so far found it convenient to establish a truth and reconciliation commission of its own, which means that it is less ready at present to face its historical responsibility than are the countries once derided as "banana republics."

All of the above-cited crimes, and many more besides, were committed on Kissinger's "watch" as secretary of state. And all of them were and are punishable, under local or international law, or both. It can hardly be argued, by himself or by his defenders, that he was indifferent to, or unaware of, the true situation. In 1999 a secret memorandum was declassified, giving excruciating details of a private conversation between Kissinger and Pinochet in Santiago, Chile, on 8 June 1976. The meeting took place the day before Kissinger was due to address the Organization of American States. The subject was human rights. Kissinger was at some pains to explain to Pinochet that the few *pro forma* remarks he was to make on that topic were by no means to be taken seriously. My friend Peter Kornbluh has performed the service of comparing the "Memcon" (Memorandum of Conversation) with the account of the meeting given by Kissinger himself in his third volume of apologia, *Years of Renewal*:

> *The Memoir*: "A considerable amount of time in my dialogue with Pinochet was devoted to human rights, which were, in fact, the principal obstacle to close United States relations with Chile. I outlined the main points in my speech to the OAS which I would deliver the next day. Pinochet made no comment."
>
> *The Memcon*: "I will treat human rights in general terms, and human rights in a world context. I will refer in two paragraphs to the report on Chile of the OAS Human Rights Commission. I will say that the human rights issue has impaired relations between the US and Chile. This is partly the result of Congressional actions. I will add that I hope you will shortly remove these

obstacles. . . . I can do no less, without producing a reaction in the US which would lead to legislative restrictions. The speech is not aimed at Chile. I wanted to tell you about this. My evaluation is that you are a victim of all left-wing groups around the world and that your greatest sin was that you overthrew a government that was going Communist."

The Memoir: "As Secretary of State, I felt I had the responsibility to encourage the Chilean government in the direction of greater democracy through a policy of understanding Pinochet's concerns. . . . Pinochet reminded me that 'Russia supports their people 100 percent. We are behind you. You are the leader. But you have a punitive system for your friends.' I returned to my underlying theme that any major help from us would realistically depend on progress on human rights."

The Memcon: "There is merit in what you say. It is a curious time in the US. . . . It is unfortunate. We have been through Vietnam and Watergate. We have to wait until the [1976] elections. We welcomed the overthrow of the Communist-inclined government here. We are not out to weaken your position."

In an unpleasant way, Pinochet twice mentioned the name of Orlando Letelier, the exiled Chilean opposition leader, accusing him of misleading the United States Congress. Kissinger's response, as can be seen, was to apologize for the Congress and (in a minor replay of his 1968 Paris tactic over Vietnam) to suggest that the dictator should hope for better days after the upcoming elections. Three months later, a car bomb in Washington killed Letelier; today still it remains the only such outrage ever committed in the nation's capital by agents of a foreign regime. (This notable incident is completely absent from Kissinger's memoirs.) The man responsible for arranging the crime, the Chilean secret policeman General Manuel Contreras, has since testified at trial that he took no action without specific and personal orders from Pinochet. He remains in prison, doubtless wondering why he trusted his superiors.

"I want to see our relations and friendship improve," Kissinger told Pinochet (but not the readers of his memoirs). "We want to help, not undermine you." In advising a murderer and despot, whose rule he had helped impose, to disregard his upcoming remarks as a sop to Congress, Kissinger insulted democracy in both countries. He also gave the greenest of green lights to further cross-border and internal terrorism, of neither of which he could have been unaware. (In his memoirs, he does mention what he calls Pinochet's "*counterterrorist* intelligence agency.") Further colluding with Pinochet against the United States Congress, which was considering the Kennedy amendment cutting off arms sales to human rights violators, Kissinger obsequiously remarked:

> I don't know if you listen in on my phone, but if you do, you have just heard me issue instructions to Washington to [defeat the Kennedy amendment]. If we defeat it, we will deliver the F-5Es as we agreed to do.

The above passage is worth bearing in mind. It is a good key for decoding the usual relationship between fact and falsehood in Kissinger's ill-crafted memoir. (And it is a huge reproach to his editors at Simon and Schuster, and Weidenfeld and Nicolson.) It should also act as an urgent prompting to members of Congress, and to human rights organizations, to reopen the incomplete inquiries and thwarted investigations into the multifarious crimes of this period. Finally, and read in the light of the return to democracy in Chile, and the decision of the Chilean courts to pursue truth and justice, it repudiates Kissinger's patronizing insult concerning the "irresponsibility" of a dignified and humane people, who have suffered very much more than verbal insult at his hands.

6

AN AFTERWORD ON CHILE

A RULE OF thumb in Washington holds that any late disclosure by offi-
cialdom will contain material that is worse than even the cynics suspected.
One need not try and turn this maxim into an iron law. However, in
September 2000 the CIA disgorged the results of an internal inquiry on
Chile, which had been required of it by the Hinchey amendment to the
Intelligence Authorization Act for that fiscal year. And the most hardened
critics and investigators were reduced to amazement. (The document was
handed to me after I had completed the chapter above, and I let it stand so
as to preserve the actual order of disclosure.) I reproduce the chief headings
below, so as to preserve, also, the Agency's own prose:

> *Support for Coup in 1970.* Under "Track II" of the strategy, CIA sought to
> instigate a coup to prevent Allende from taking office after he won a plural-
> ity in the 4 September election and before, as Constitutionally required
> because he did not win an absolute majority, the Chilean Congress reaf-
> firmed his victory. CIA was working with three different groups of plotters.
> All three groups made it clear that any coup would require the kidnapping of
> Army Commander René Schneider, who felt deeply that the Constitution
> required that the Army allow Allende to assume power. CIA agreed with that
> assessment. Although CIA provided weapons to one of the groups, we have
> found no information that the plotters' or CIA's intention was for the general

to be killed. Contact with one group of plotters was dropped early on because of its extremist tendencies. CIA provided tear gas, submachine guns and ammunition to the second group, mortally wounding him in the attack. CIA had previously encouraged this group to launch a coup but withdrew support four days before the attack because, in CIA's assessment, the group could not carry it out successsfully.

This repeats the old canard supposedly distinguishing a kidnap or abduction from a murder, and once again it raises the intriguing question: what was the CIA going to do with the general once it had kidnapped him? (Note, also, the studied passivity whereby the report "found no information that the plotters' or CIA's intention was for the general to be killed." What would satisfy this bizarre criterion?) But then we learn, of the supposedly unruly gang that actually took its instructions seriously:

> In November 1970 a member of the Viaux group who avoided capture recontacted the Agency and requested financial assistance on behalf of the group. Although the Agency had no obligation to the group because it acted on its own, in an effort to keep the prior contact secret, maintain the good will of the group, and for humanitarian reasons, $35,000 was passed.

"Humanitarian reasons." One has to admire the sheer inventiveness of this explanation. At 1970 prices, the sum of $35,000 in Chile was a considerable sum to pay. Not the sort of sum that a local station chief could have disbursed on his own. One wants to know how the Forty Committee and its vigilant chairman, Henry Kissinger, decided that the best way to dissociate from a supposedly loose-cannon gang was to pay it a small fortune in cash *after* it had committed a cold-blooded murder.

The same question arises in an even more acute form with another disclosure made by the Agency in the course of the same report. This is headed "Relationship With Contreras." Manuel Contreras was the head of Pinochet's secret military police, and in that capacity organized the death, torture, and disappearance of innumerable Chileans as well as the use of bombing and assassination techniques as far afield as Washington, DC.

The CIA admits early on in the document that it "had liaison relationships in Chile with the primary purpose of securing assistance in gathering intelligence on external targets. The CIA offered these service assistance in internal organization and training to combat subversion and terrorism abroad, not in combating internal opponents of the government."

Such flat prose, based on a distinction between the "external threat" and the more messy business of internal dictatorial discipline, invites the question – what external threat? Chile had no foreign enemy except Argentina, which disputed some sea lane rights in the Beagle Channel. (In consequence, Chile helped Mrs Thatcher in the Falklands war of 1982.) And in Argentina, as we know, the CIA was likewise engaged in helping the military regime to survive. No: while Chile had no external enemies to speak of, the Pinochet dictatorship had many, many external foes. They were the numerous Chileans forced to abandon their country. One of the jobs of Manuel Contreras was to hunt them down. As the report puts it:

> During a period between 1974 and 1977, CIA maintained contact with Manuel Contreras, who later became notorious for his human rights abuses. The US Government policy community approved CIA's contact with Contreras, given his position as chief of the primary intelligence organization in Chile, as necessary to accomplish the CIA's mission, in spite of concerns that this relationship might lay the CIA open to charges of aiding internal political repression.

After a few bits of back-and-forth about the distinction without a difference (between external and "internal" police tactics) the CIA report states candidly:

> By April 1975, intelligence reporting showed that Contreras was the principal obstacle to a reasonable human rights policy within the Junta, but an interagency committee directed the CIA to continue its relationship with Contreras. The US Ambassador to Chile urged Deputy Director of Central Intelligence [General Vernon] Walters to receive Contreras in Washington in the interests of maintaining good relations with Pinochet. In August 1975, with interagency approval, this meeting took place.

In May and June 1975, elements within the CIA recommended establishing a paid relationship with Contreras to obtain intelligence based on his unique position and access to Pinochet. This proposal was overruled, citing the US Government policy on clandestine relations with the head of an intelligence service notorious for human rights abuses. However, given miscommunications in the timing of this exchange, a one-time payment was given to Contreras.

This does not require too much parsing. Some time *after* it had been concluded, and by the CIA at that, that Manuel Contreras was the "principal obstacle to a reasonable human rights policy," he is given American taxpayers' money and received at a high level in Washington. The CIA's memorandum is careful to state that, where doubts exist, they are stilled by "the US Government policy community" and by "an interagency committee." It also tries to suggest, with unconscious humor, that the head of a murderous foreign secret service was given a large bribe by mistake. One wonders who was reprimanded for this blunder, and how it got past the scrutiny of the Forty Committee.

The report also contradicts itself, stating at one point that Contreras's activities overseas were opaque, and at another that:

Within a year after the coup, the CIA and other US Government agencies were aware of bilateral cooperation among regional intelligence services to track the activities of and, in at least a few cases, kill political opponents. This was the precursor to Operation Condor, an intelligence-sharing arrangement among Chile, Argentina, Brazil, Paraguay and Uruguay established in 1975.

So now we know: the internationalization of the death squad principle was understood and approved by US intelligence and its political masters across two administrations. The senior person concerned in both administrations was Henry Kissinger. Whichever "interagency committee" is meant, and whether it is the Forty Committee or the Interagency Committee on Chile, the traces lead back to the same source.

On leaving the State Department, Kissinger made an extraordinary bargain whereby (having first hastily trucked them for safekeeping on the Rockefeller estate at Pocantico Hills, New York) he gifted his papers to the Library of Congress, on the sole condition that they remained under seal until after his demise. However, Kissinger's friend Manuel Contreras made a mistake when he killed a United States citizen, Ronni Karpen Moffitt, in the Washington car bomb which also murdered Orlando Letelier in 1976. By late 2000, the FBI had finally sought and received subpoena power to review the Library of Congress papers, a subpoena with which Kissinger dealt only through his attorneys. It was a start, but it was pathetic when compared to the efforts of truth and justice commissions in "Chile, Argentina, Brazil, Paraguay and Uruguay," the nations named above, which have now emerged from years of Kissinger-befriended dictatorship and sought a full accounting. We await the moment when the United States Congress will inaugurate a comparable process, and finally subpoena all the hidden documents that obscure the view of unpunished crimes committed in our names.

7

CYPRUS

IN THE SECOND volume of his trilogy of memoirs, which is entitled *Years of Upheaval*, Henry Kissinger found the subject of the 1974 Cyprus catastrophe so awkward that he decided to postpone consideration of it:

> I must leave a full discussion of the Cyprus episode to another occasion, for it stretched into the Ford presidency and its legacy exists unresolved today.

This argued a certain nervousness on his part, if only because the subjects of Vietnam, Cambodia, the Middle East, Angola, Chile, China and the SALT negotiations all bear legacies that are "unresolved today" and were unresolved then. (To say that these matters "stretched into the Ford administration" is to say, in effect, nothing at all except that this pallid interregnum did, historically speaking, occur.)

In most of his writing about himself (and, one presumes, in most of his presentations to his clients) Kissinger projects a strong impression of a man at home in the world and on top of his brief. But there are a number of occasions when it suits him to pose as a sort of Candide: naive, and ill-prepared for and easily unhorsed by events. No doubt this pose costs him something in point of self-esteem. It is a pose, furthermore, which he often adopts at precisely the time when the record shows him to be knowledgeable, and when knowledge or foreknowledge would also confront him with charges of responsibility or complicity.

Cyprus in 1974 is just such a case. Kissinger now argues, in the long-delayed third volume of his memoirs, *Years of Renewal*, that he was prevented and distracted, by Watergate and the deliquescence of the Nixon presidency, from taking a timely or informed interest in the crucial triangle of force between Greece, Turkey and Cyprus. This is a bizarre disclaimer: the phrase "southern flank of NATO" was then a geopolitical commonplace of the first importance, and the proximity of Cyprus to the Middle East was a factor never absent from US strategic thinking. There was no reason of domestic policy to prevent the region from engaging his attention. Furthermore, the very implosion of Nixonian authority, cited as a reason for Kissinger's own absence of mind, in fact bestowed extraordinary powers upon him. To restate the obvious once more: when he became secretary of state in 1973, he took care to retain his post as Special Assistant to the President for National Security Affairs or, as we now say, National Security Advisor. This made him the first and only secretary of state to hold the chairmanship of the elite and secretive Forty Committee, which considered and approved covert actions by the CIA. Meanwhile, as chairman of the National Security Council, he held a position where every important intelligence plan passed across his desk. His former NSC aide, Roger Morris, was not exaggerating by much, if at all, when he said that Kissinger's dual position, plus Nixon's eroded status, made him "no less than acting chief of state for national security."

We know from other sources that Kissinger was not only a micromanager with an eye to detail, but a man with a taste for intervention and rapid response. In the White House memoir of one of his closest associates, Nixon's chief of staff H.R. Haldeman, we learn of an occasion when Kissinger nearly precipitated a crisis because he became excited by some aerial photographs of Cuba. (The pictures showed soccer fields under construction, which he took – believing the Cubans to be exclusively interested in baseball – as the sign of a new and sinister Russian design.) On another occasion, following the downing of a US plane, he was in favor of bombing North Korea and not excluding the nuclear option. *The Ends of Power* was

Haldeman's title; it is only one of many testimonies showing Kissinger's unsleeping attention to potential sources of trouble, and therefore of possible distinction for himself.

This is a necessary preface to a consideration of his self-exculpation in the Cyprus matter, an apologia which depends for its credibility on our willingness to believe that Kissinger was wholly incompetent and impotent and above all uninformed. The energy with which he presses this self-abnegating case is revealing. It is also important, because if Kissinger did have any knowledge of the events he describes, then he is guilty of collusion in an assassination attempt on a foreign head of state, in a fascist military coup, in a serious violation of American law (the Foreign Assistance Act, which prohibits the use of US military aid and *materiel* for non-defensive purposes), in two invasions which flouted international law, and in the murder and dispossession of many thousands of noncombatant civilians.

In seeking to fend off this conclusion, and its implications, Kissinger gives one hostage to fortune in *Years of Upheaval* and another in *Years of Renewal*. In the former volume he says plainly, "I had always taken it for granted that the next intercommunal crisis in Cyprus would provoke Turkish intervention," that is, it would at least risk the prospect of a war within NATO between Greece and Turkey and would certainly involve the partition of the island. That this was indeed common knowledge may not be doubted by any person even lightly acquainted with Cypriot affairs. In the latter volume, where he finally takes up the challenge implicitly refused in the former, he repeatedly asks the reader why anyone (such as himself, so burdened with Watergate) would have sought "a crisis in the Eastern Mediterranean between two NATO allies."

These two disingenuous statements need to be qualified in the light of a third, which appears on page 199 of *Years of Renewal*. Here, President Makarios of Cyprus is described without adornment as "the proximate cause of most of Cyprus's tensions." Makarios was the democratically elected leader of a virtually unarmed republic, which was at the time an associate member of the European Economic Community (EEC), the

United Nations and the Commonwealth. His rule was challenged, and the independence of Cyprus was threatened, by a military dictatorship in Athens and a highly militarized government in Turkey, both of which sponsored right-wing gangster organizations on the island, and both of which had plans to annex the greater or lesser part of it. In spite of this, "intercommunal" violence had been on the decline in Cyprus throughout the 1970s. Most killings were in fact "intramural": of Greek and Turkish democrats or internationalists by their respective nationalist and authoritarian rivals. Several attempts, by Greek and Greek-Cypriot fanatics, had been made on the life of President Makarios himself. To describe his person as "the proximate cause" of most of the tensions is to make a wildly aberrant moral judgment.

This same aberrant judgment, however, supplies the key that unlocks the lie at the heart of Kissinger's presentation. If the elected civilian authority (and spiritual leader of the Greek Orthodox community) is the "proximate cause" of the tensions, then his removal from the scene is self-evidently the cure for them. If one can demonstrate that there was such a removal plan, and that Kissinger knew about it in advance, then it follows logically and naturally that he was not ostensibly looking for a crisis – as he self-pityingly asks us to disbelieve – but for a solution. The fact that he got a crisis, which was also a hideous calamity for Cyprus and the region, does not change the equation or undo the syllogism. It is attributable to the other observable fact that the scheme to remove Makarios, on which the "solution" depended, was in practice a failure. But those who willed the means and wished the ends are not absolved from guilt by the refusal of reality to match their schemes.

It is, from Kissinger's own record and recollection, as well as from the record of the subsequent official inquiry, quite easy to demonstrate that he did have advance knowledge of the plan to depose and kill Makarios. He admits as much himself, by noting that the Greek dictator Dimitrios Ioannides, head of the secret police, was determined to mount a coup in Cyprus and bring the island under the control of Athens. This was one of the better-known facts of the situation, as was the more embarrassing fact that Brigadier Ioannides was dependent on US military aid and political sympathy. His police state had been expelled from the Council of Europe and blocked from joining the EEC, and it was largely the advantage conferred by his agreement to "home port" the US Sixth Fleet, and host a string of US air and intelligence bases, that kept him in power. This lenient policy was highly controversial in Congress and in the American press, and the argument over it was part of Kissinger's daily bread long before the Watergate drama.

Thus it was understood *in general* that the Greek dictatorship, a US client, wished to see Makarios overthrown and had already tried to kill him or have him killed. (Overthrow and assassination, incidentally, are effectively coterminous in this account; there was no possibility of leaving such a charismatic leader alive, and those who sought his removal invariably intended his death.) This was also understood *in particular*. The most salient proof is this. In May of 1974, two months before the coup in Nicosia which Kissinger later claimed was a shock, he received a memorandum from the head of his State Department Cyprus desk, Thomas Boyatt. Boyatt summarized all the cumulative and persuasive reasons for believing that a Greek junta attack on Cyprus and Makarios was imminent. He further argued that, in the absence of a US démarche to Athens, warning the dictators to desist, it might be assumed that the United States was indifferent to this. And he added what everybody knew – that such a coup, if it went forward, would beyond doubt trigger a Turkish invasion.

Prescient memos are a dime a dozen in Washington after a crisis; they are often then read for the first time, or leaked to the press or Congress in order to enhance (or protect) some bureaucratic reputation. But Kissinger now admits that he saw this document in real time, while engaged in his shuttle between Syria and Israel (both of them within half an hour's flying time of Cyprus). Yet no démarche bearing his name or carrying his authority was issued to the Greek junta.

A short while afterwards, on 7 June 1974, the *National Intelligence Daily*, which is the breakfast/bible reading of all senior State Department, Pentagon and national security officials, quoted a US field report dated 3 June which stated the views of the dictator in Athens:

> Ioannides claimed that Greece is capable of removing Makarios and his key supporters from power in twenty-four hours with little if any blood being shed and without EOKA assistance. The Turks would quietly acquiesce to the removal of Makarios, a key enemy. . . . Ioannides stated that if Makarios decided on some type of extreme provocation against Greece to obtain a tactical advantage, he is not sure whether he should merely pull the Greek troops out of Cyprus and let Makarios fend for himself, or remove Makarios once and for all and have Greece deal directly with Turkey over Cyprus's future.

This report and its contents were later authenticated before Congress by CIA staff who had served in Athens at the relevant time. The fact that it made Brigadier Ioannides seem bombastic and delusional – both of which he was – should have underlined the obvious and imminent danger. (EOKA was a Greek-Cypriot fascist underground, armed and paid by the junta.)

At about the same time, Kissinger received a call from Senator J. William Fulbright, the chairman of the Senate Foreign Relations Committee. Senator Fulbright had been briefed about the impending coup by a senior Greek dissident journalist in Washington named Elias P. Demetracopoulos. He told Kissinger that steps should be taken to avert the planned Greek action, and he gave three reasons. The first was that it would repair some of the moral damage done by the US government's indulgence of the junta. The second was that it would head off a confrontation between Greece and Turkey in the Mediterranean. The third was that it would enhance US prestige on the island. Kissinger declined to take the recommended steps, on the bizarre grounds that he could not intervene in Greek "internal affairs" at a time when the Nixon administration was resisting pressure from Senator Henry Jackson to link US–Soviet trade to the free emigration of

Russian Jewry. However odd this line of argument, it still makes it impossible for Kissinger to claim, as he still does, that he had had no warning.

So there was still no high-level US concern registered with Athens. The difficulty is sometimes presented as one of protocol or etiquette, as if Kissinger's regular custom was to whisper and tread lightly. Ioannides was the *de facto* head of the regime but technically only its secret police chief. For the US ambassador, Henry Tasca, it was awkward to make diplomatic approaches to a man he described as "a cop." But again I remind you that Henry Kissinger, in addition to his formal diplomatic eminence, was also head of the Forty Committee, and supervisor of covert action, and was dealing in private with an Athens regime that had long-standing CIA ties. The 1976 House Committee on Intelligence later phrased the problem rather deftly in its report:

> Tasca, assured by the CIA station chief that Ioannides would *continue* to deal only with the CIA, and not sharing the State Department Desk Officer's alarm, was content to pass a message to the Greek leader indirectly. . . . It is clear, however, that the embassy took no steps to underscore for Ioannides the depth of concern over a Cyprus coup attempt. This episode, the exclusive CIA access to Ioannides, Tasca's indications that he may not have seen all important messages to and from the CIA station, Ioannides' suggestions of US acquiescence, and Washington's well-known coolness to Makarios have led to public speculation that either US officials were inattentive to the reports of the developing crisis or simply allowed it to happen.

Thomas Boyatt's memoranda, warning of precisely what was to happen (and echoing the views of several mid-level officials besides himself), were classified as secret and have still never been released. Asked to testify at the above hearings, he was at first forbidden by Kissinger to appear before Congress. He was only finally permitted to do so in order that he might avoid a citation for contempt. His evidence was taken in "executive session," with the hearing-room cleared of staff, reporters, and visitors.

Events continued to gather pace. On 1 July 1974, three senior officials of the Greek foreign ministry, all of them known for their moderate views on the Cyprus question, publicly tendered their resignations. On 3 July President Makarios made public an open letter to the Greek junta, which made the direct accusation of foreign interference and subversion:

> In order to be absolutely clear, I say that the cadres of the military regime of Greece support and direct the activities of the EOKA-B terrorists. . . . I have more than once so far felt, and in some cases I have touched, a hand invisibly extending from Athens and seeking to liquidate my human existence.

He called for the withdrawal from Cyprus of the Greek officers responsible.

Some days after the coup, which eventually occurred on 15 July 1974, and when challenged at a press conference about his apparent failure to foresee or avert it, Kissinger replied that "the information was not lying around in the streets." Actually, it almost was in the streets. But much more important, and much more material to the case, it had been available to him round the clock, in both his diplomatic and his intelligence capacities. His decision to do nothing was therefore a direct decision to do something, or to let something be done.

The argument can be pushed a little further. If we can show that Kissinger is speaking falsely when he says he was surprised by the July coup – and we can show this – and if we assume that foreknowledge accompanied by inaction is evidence for at least passive approval, then we would expect to find the coup, when it came, being received with some show of sympathy or satisfaction. As a matter of fact, that is precisely what we do find.

To the rest of the world, two things were obvious about the coup. The first was that it had been instigated from Athens and carried out with the help of regular Greek forces, and was thus a direct intervention in the internal affairs of one country by another. The second was that it violated all the existing treaties governing the status of Cyprus. The obvious and unsavory illegality was luridly emphasized by the junta itself, which chose a notorious chauvinist gunman named Nicos Sampson to be its proxy "president." Sampson must have been well known to the chairman of the

Forty Committee as a long-standing recipient of financial support from the CIA; he also received money for his fanatical Nicosia newspaper *Makhi* (Combat) from a pro-junta CIA proxy in Athens, Mr Savvas Constantopoulos, the publisher of the pro-junta organ *Eleftheros Kosmos* (Free World). No European government treated Sampson as anything but a pariah, for the brief nine days in which he held power and launched a campaign of murder against his democratic Greek opponents. But Kissinger told the US envoy in Nicosia to receive Sampson's "foreign minister" *as* foreign minister, thus making the United States the first and only government to extend *de facto* recognition. (At this point, it might be emphasized, the whereabouts of President Makarios were unknown. His palace had been heavily shelled and his death announced on the junta's radio. He had in fact made his escape, and was able to broadcast the fact a few days afterwards – to the enormous irritation of certain well-placed persons.) Incidentally, in his 1986 memoir *The Truth*, published in Athens in 1986, the then head of the Greek armed forces, General Grigorios Bonanos, records that the junta's attack on Cyprus brought a message of approval and support, delivered to its intelligence service by no less a man than Thomas A. Pappas himself – the chosen intermediary between the junta and the Nixon–Kissinger administration. (We shall hear more about Mr Pappas in Chapter 9.)

In Washington, Kissinger's press spokesman Robert Anderson flatly denied that the coup – later described by Makarios from the podium of the United Nations as "an invasion" – constituted foreign intervention. "No," he replied to a direct question on this point. "In our view there has been no outside intervention." This surreal position was not contradicted by Kissinger when he met with the ambassador of Cyprus and failed to offer the customary condolences on the reported death of his president – the "proximate cause," we now learn from him, of all the unpleasantness. When asked if he still recognized the elected Makarios government as the legal one, Kissinger doggedly and astonishingly refused to answer. When asked if the United States was moving towards recognition of the Sampson regime, his spokesman declined to deny it. When Makarios came to Washington on 22 July, the State Department was asked whether he would be received by Kissinger "as a private citizen, as Archbishop, or as President of Cyprus?" The answer? "He [Kissinger] is meeting with *Archbishop* Makarios on Monday [emphasis added]." Every other government in the world, save the rapidly collapsing Greek dictatorship, recognized Makarios as the legitimate head of the Cyprus republic. Kissinger's unilateralism on the point is without diplomatic precedent, and argues strongly for his collusion and sympathy with the armed handful of thugs who felt the same way.

It is worth emphasizing that Makarios was invited to Washington in the first place, as elected and legal president of Cyprus, by Senator J. William Fulbright of the Senate Foreign Relations Committee and by his counterpart Congressman Thomas Morgan, chairman of the House Foreign Affairs Committee. Credit for this invitation belongs to the above-mentioned Elias Demetracopoulos, who had long warned of the coup and who was a friend of Fulbright. He it was who conveyed the invitation to Makarios, who was by then in London meeting the British Foreign Secretary. This initiative crowned a series of anti-junta activities by this guerrilla journalist and one-man band, who had already profoundly irritated Kissinger and become a special object of his spite. (See Chapter 9.) At the very last moment, and with very poor grace, Kissinger was compelled to announce that he was receiving Makarios in his presidential and not his episcopal capacity.

Since Kissinger himself tells us that he had always known or assumed that another outbreak of violence in Cyprus would trigger a Turkish military intervention, we can assume in our turn that he was not surprised when such an intervention came. Nor does he seem to have been very much disconcerted. While the Greek junta remained in power, his efforts were principally directed to shielding it from retaliation. He was opposed to the return of Makarios to the island, and strongly opposed to Turkish or British use of force (Britain being a guarantor power with a treaty obligation and troops in place on Cyprus) to undo the Greek coup. This same counsel of inertia or inaction – amply testified to in his own memoirs as well as in everyone else's – translated later into equally strict and repeated admonitions against any measures to block a Turkish invasion. Sir Tom McNally, then the chief political advisor to Britain's then Foreign Secretary and future prime minister, James Callaghan, has since disclosed that Kissinger "vetoed" at least one British military action to preempt a Turkish landing. But that was *after* the Greek colonels had collapsed, and democracy had been restored to Athens. There was no longer a client regime to protect.

This may seem paradoxical, but the long-standing sympathy for a partition of Cyprus, repeatedly expressed by the State and Defense departments, make it seem much less so. The demographic composition of the island (82 percent Greek to 18 percent Turkish) made it more logical for the partition to be imposed by Greece. But a second-best was to have it imposed by Turkey. And, once Turkey had conducted two brutal invasions and occupied almost 40 percent of Cypriot territory, Kissinger exerted himself very strongly indeed to protect Ankara from any congressional reprisal for this outright violation of international law, and promiscuous and illegal misuse of US weaponry. He became so pro-Turkish, indeed, that it was if he had never heard of the Greek colonels. (Though his expressed dislike of the returned Greek democratic leaders supplied an occasional reminder.)

Not all the elements of this partitionist policy can be charged to Kissinger personally; he inherited the Greek junta and the official dislike of Makarios. However, even in the dank obfuscatory prose of his own memoirs, he does admit what can otherwise be concluded from independent sources. Using covert channels, and short-circuiting the democratic process in his own country, he made himself an accomplice in a plan of political assassination which, when it went awry, led to the deaths of thousands of civilians, the violent uprooting of almost 200,000 refugees, and the creation of an unjust and unstable amputation of Cyprus which constitutes a serious threat to peace a full quarter-century later. His attempts to keep the record sealed are significant in themselves; when the relevant files are opened they will form part of the longer bill of indictment.

On 10 July 1976, the European Commission on Human Rights adopted a report, prepared by eighteen distinguished jurists and chaired by Professor J.E.S. Fawcett, resulting from a year's research into the consequences of the Turkish invasion. It found that the Turkish army had engaged in the deliberate killing of civilians, in the execution of prisoners, in the torture and ill-treatment of detainees, in the arbitrary collective punishment and mass detention of civilians, and in systematic and unpunished acts of rape, torture, and looting. A large number of "disappeared" persons, both prisoners of war and civilians, are still "missing" from this period. They include a dozen holders of United States passports, which is evidence in itself of an indiscriminate strategy, when conducted by an army dependent on US aid and *materiel*.

Perhaps it was a reluctance to accept his responsibility for these outrages, as well as his responsibility for the original Sampson coup, that led Kissinger to tell a bizarre sequence of lies to his new friends the Chinese. On 2 October 1974, he held a high-level meeting in New York with Qiao Guanhua, Vice Foreign Minister of the People's Republic. It was the first substantive Sino–American meeting since the visit of Deng Xiaoping, and the first order of business was Cyprus. The memorandum, which is headed "TOP SECRET/SENSITIVE/EXCLUSIVELY EYES ONLY," has Kissinger first rejecting China's public claim that he had helped engineer the removal of Makarios. "We did not. We did not oppose Makarios." (This claim is directly belied by his own memoirs.) He says, "When the coup occurred I was in Moscow," which he was not. He says, "my people did not take these intelligence reports [concerning an impending coup] seriously," even though they had. He says that neither did Makarios take them seriously, even though Makarios had gone public in a denunciation of the Athens junta for its coup plans. Kissinger then makes the amazing claim "We knew the Soviets had told the Turks to invade," which would make this the first Soviet-instigated invasion to be conducted by a NATO army and paid for with US aid.

A good liar must have a good memory: Kissinger is a stupendous liar with a remarkable memory. So perhaps some of this hysterical lying is explained by its context – by the need to enlist China's anti-Soviet instincts. But the total of falsity is so impressive that it suggests something additional, something more like denial or delusion, or even a confession by other means.

8

EAST TIMOR

ANOTHER SMALL BUT significant territory has the distinction of being omitted – entirely omitted – from Henry Kissinger's memoirs. And since East Timor is left out of the third and final volume (*Years of Renewal*) it cannot hope, like Cyprus, for a hasty later emendation. It has, in short, been airbrushed. And it is reasonably easy to see why Kissinger hopes to avoid discussion of a country whose destiny he so much affected.

Let me state matters briefly. After the collapse of the Portuguese fascist regime in Lisbon in April 1974, that country's colonial empire deliquesced with extraordinary speed. The metropolitan power retained control only in the enclave of Macau, on the coast of China, and later remitted this territory to Beijing under treaty in 2000. In Africa, after many vicissitudes, power was inherited by the socialist-leaning liberation movements which had, by their tactic of guerrilla warfare, brought about the Portuguese revolution in the first place and established warm relations with its first generation of activists.

In East Timor, situated in the Indonesian archipelago, the postcolonial vacuum was at first also filled by a leftist movement, known as FRETILIN or the Front for the Liberation of East Timor. The popular base of this movement extended from the Catholic Church to the Westernized and sometimes Leninized students who had brought back revolutionary opinions from the "motherland." FRETILIN and its allies were able to form a government but were at once subjected to exorbitant pressure from their gigantic Indonesian neighbor, then led by the dictator (since deposed and disgraced by his own people) General Suharto. Portugal, which had and which retains legal responsibility, was too unstable and too distant to prevent the infiltration of Indonesian regular units into East Timor and the beginning of an obviously expansionist policy of attrition and subversion. This tactic was pursued by the generals in Jakarta for a few months, under the transparent pretext of "aiding" anti-FRETILIN forces which were, in point of fact, deliberately inserted Indonesian ones. All pretense of this sort was abandoned on 7 December 1975, when the armed forces of Indonesia crossed the border of East Timor in strength, eventually proclaiming it (in an act no less lawless than Iraq's proclamation of Kuwait as "our nineteenth province") a full part of Indonesia proper.

Timorese resistance to this claim was so widespread, and the violence required to impose it was so ruthless and generalized, that the figure of 100,000 deaths in the first wave – perhaps one-sixth of the entire population – is reckoned an understatement.

The date of the Indonesian invasion – 7 December 1975 – is of importance and also of significance. On that date, President Gerald Ford and his secretary of state, Henry Kissinger, concluded an official visit to Jakarta and flew to Hawaii. Since they had come fresh from a meeting with Indonesia's military junta, and since the United States was Indonesia's principal supplier of military hardware (and since Portugal, a NATO ally, broke diplomatic relations with Indonesia on the point), it seemed reasonable to inquire whether the two leaders had given the invaders any impression amounting to a "green light." Thus when Ford and Kissinger landed at Hawaii, reporters asked Mr Ford for comment on the invasion of Timor. The President was evasive.

> He smiled and said: "We'll talk about that later." But press secretary Ron Nessen later gave reporters a statement saying: "The United States is always concerned about the use of violence. The President hopes it can be resolved peacefully."

The literal incoherence of this official utterance – the idea of a peaceful resolution to a unilateral use of violence – may perhaps have possessed an
inner coherence: the hope of a speedy victory for overwhelming force.
Kissinger moved this suspicion a shade nearer to actualization in his own
more candid comment, which was offered while he was still on Indonesian
soil and "told newsmen in Jakarta that the United States would not recognize the FRETILIN-declared republic and that 'the United States
understands Indonesia's position on the question.'"

So gruesome were the subsequent reports of mass slaughter, rape, and
deliberate use of starvation that such bluntness fell somewhat out of fashion. The killing of several Australian journalists who had witnessed
Indonesia's atrocities, the devastation in the capital city of Dili, and the
stubbornness of FRETILIN's hugely outgunned rural resistance made East
Timor an embarrassment rather than an advertisement for Jakarta's new
order. Kissinger generally attempted to avoid any discussion of his involvement in the extirpation of the Timorese – an ongoing involvement, since he
authorized back-door shipments of weapons to those doing the extirpat-
ing – and was ably seconded in this by his ambassador to the United
Nations, Daniel Patrick Moynihan, who later confided in his memoir *A
Dangerous Place* that, in relative terms, the death toll in East Timor during
the initial days of the invasion was "almost the toll of casualties experienced
by the Soviet Union during the Second World War." Moynihan continued:

> The United States wished things to turn out as they did, and worked to
> bring this about. The Department of State desired that the United Nations
> prove utterly ineffective in whatever measures it undertook. This task was
> given to me, and I carried it forward with no inconsiderable success.

The terms "United States" and "Department of State" are here foully pros-
tituted, by this supposed prose-master, since they are used as synonyms for
Henry Kissinger.

Twenty years later, on 11 August 1995, Kissinger was confronted with
direct questions on the subject. Publicizing and promoting his then-latest

book *Diplomacy*, at an event sponsored by the Learning Exchange at the Park Central Hotel in New York, he perhaps (having omitted Timor from his book and from his talk) did not anticipate the first line of questioning that arose from the floor. Constancio Pinto, a former resistance leader in Timor who had been captured and tortured and had escaped to the United States, was first on his feet:

Pinto: I am Timorese. My name is Constancio Pinto. And I followed your speech today and it's really interesting. One thing that I know you didn't mention is this place invaded by Indonesia in 1975. It is in Southeast Asia. As a result of the invasion 200,000 people of the Timorese were killed. As far as I know Dr Kissinger was in Indonesia the day before the invasion of East Timor. The United States actually supported Indonesia in East Timor. So I would like to know what you were doing at that time.

Kissinger: What was I doing at that time? The whole time or just about Timor? First of all, I want to thank the gentleman for asking the question in a very polite way. The last time somebody from Timor came after me was at the Oxford Union and they practically tore the place apart before they asked the question.

What most people who deal with government don't understand is one of the most overwhelming experiences of being in high office. That there are always more problems than you can possibly address at any one period. And when you're in global policy and you're a global power, there are so many issues.

Now the Timor issue. First of all you have to understand what Timor, what Timor, what the issue of Timor is. Every island that was occupied by the Dutch in the colonial period was constituted as the Republic of Indonesia. In the middle of their archipelago was an island called Timor. Or is an island called Timor. Half of it was Indonesian and the other half of it was Portuguese. This was the situation.

Now I don't want to offend the gentleman who asked the question.

We had so many problems to deal with. We had at that time, there was a war going on in Angola. We had just been driven out of Vietnam. We were conducting negotiations in the Middle East, and Lebanon had blown up. We were on a trip to China. Maybe regrettably we weren't even thinking about Timor. I'm telling you what the truth of the matter is. The reason we were in Indonesia was actually accidental. We had originally intended to go to China, we meaning President Ford and myself and some others. We had originally intended to go to China for five days. This was the period when Mao was very sick and there had been an upheaval in China. The so-called Gang of Four was becoming dominant and we had a terrible time agreeing with the Chinese, where to go, what to say. So we cut our trip to China short. We went for two days to China and then we went for a day and a half to the Philippines and a day and a half to Indonesia. That's how we got to Indonesia in the first place. So this was really at that time to tell the Chinese we were not dependent on them. So that's how we got to Indonesia.

Timor was never discussed with us when we were in Indonesia. At the airport as we were leaving, the Indonesians told us that they were going to occupy the Portuguese colony of Timor. To us that did not look like a very significant event because the Indians had occupied the Portuguese colony of Goa ten years earlier and to us it looked like another process of decolonization. Nobody had the foggiest idea of what would happen afterwards, and nobody asked our opinion, and I don't know what we could have said if someone had asked our opinion. It was literally told to us as we were leaving.

Now there's been a terrible human tragedy in Timor afterwards. The population of East Timor has resisted and I don't know whether the casualty figures are correct. I just don't know, but they're certainly significant and there's no question that it's a huge tragedy. All I'm telling you is what we knew in 1975. This was not a big thing on our radar screen. Nobody has ever heard again of Goa after the Indians occupied it. And to us, Timor, look at a map, it's a little speck of an island in a huge archipelago, half of which was Portuguese. We had no reason to say the Portuguese should stay there. And so when the Indonesians informed us, we neither said yes or no. We were literally at the airport. So that was our connection with it, but I grant the questioner the fact that it's been a great tragedy.

Allan Nairn: Mr Kissinger, my name is Allan Nairn. I'm a journalist in the United States. I'm one of the Americans who survived the massacre in East Timor on November 12, 1991, a massacre during which Indonesian troops armed with American M-16s gunned down at least 271 Timorese civilians in front of the Santa Cruz Catholic cemetery as they were gathered in the act of peaceful mourning and protest. Now you just said that in your meeting with Suharto on the afternoon of December 6, 1975, you did not discuss Timor, you did not discuss it until you came to the airport. Well, I have here the official State Department transcript of your and President Ford's conversation with General Suharto, the dictator of Indonesia. It was obtained through the Freedom of Information Act. It has been edited under the Freedom of Information Act so the whole text isn't there. It's clear from the portion of the text that is here, that in fact you did discuss the impending invasion of Timor with Suharto, a fact which was confirmed to me by President Ford himself in an interview I had with him. President Ford told me that in fact you discussed the impending invasion of Timor with Suharto and that you gave the US . . .

Kissinger: Who? I or he?

Nairn: That you and President Ford together gave US approval for the invasion of East Timor. There is another internal State Department memo which is printed in an extensive excerpt here which I'll give to anyone in your audience that's interested. This is a memo of a December 18, 1975, meeting held at the State Department. This was held right after your return from that trip and you were berating your staff for having put on paper a finding by the State Department legal advisor Mr Leigh that the Indonesian invasion was illegal, that it not only violated international law, it violated a treaty with the US because US weapons were used and it's clear from this transcript which I invite anyone in the audience to peruse that you were angry at them first because you feared this memo would leak, and second because you were supporting the Indonesian invasion of East Timor, and you did not want it known that you were doing this contrary to the advice of your own people in the State Department. If one looks at the public actions, sixteen hours after you left that meeting with Suharto the Indonesian troops began parachuting over Dili, the capital of East Timor. They came ashore and began the massacres that culminated in a third of the Timorese population. You announced an immediate doubling of US military aid to Indonesia at the time, and in the meantime at the United Nations, the instruction given to Ambassador Daniel Patrick Moynihan, as he wrote in his memoirs, was to, as he put it, see to it that the UN be highly ineffective in any actions it might undertake on East Timor . . . [shouts from the audience]

Kissinger: Look, I think we all got the point now . . .

Nairn: My question, Mr Kissinger, my question, Dr Kissinger, is twofold. First will you give a waiver under the Privacy Act to support full declassification of this memo so we can see exactly what you and President Ford said to Suharto? Secondly, would you support the convening of an international war crimes tribunal under UN supervision on the subject of East Timor and would you agree to abide by its verdict in regard to your own conduct?

Kissinger: I mean, uh, really, this sort of comment is one of the reasons why the conduct of foreign policy is becoming nearly impossible under these conditions. Here is a fellow who's got one obsession, he's got one problem, he collects a bunch of documents, you don't know what is in these documents . . .

Nairn: I invite your audience to read them.

Kissinger: Well, read them. Uh, the fact is essentially as I described them [thumps podium]. Timor was not a significant American policy problem. If Suharto raised it, if Ford said something that sounded encouraging, it was not a significant American foreign policy problem. It seemed to us to be an anti-colonial problem in which the Indonesians were taking over Timor and we had absolutely no reason at that time to pay any huge attention to it.

Secondly you have to understand these things in the context of the period. Vietnam had just collapsed. Nobody yet knew what effect the domino theory would have. Indonesia was . . . is a country of a population of 160 million and the key, a key country in Southeast Asia. We were not looking for trouble with Indonesia and the reason I objected in the State Department to putting this thing on paper; it wasn't that it was put on paper. It was that it was circulated to embassies because it was guaranteed to leak out. It was guaranteed then to lead to some public confrontation and for better or worse our fundamental position on these human rights issues was always to try to see if we could discuss them first, quietly, before they turned into a public confrontation. This was our policy with respect to emigration from Russia, in which we turned out to be right, and this was the policy which we tried to pursue in respect to Indonesia and anybody can go and find some document and take out one sentence and try to prove something fundamental and now I think we've heard enough about Timor. Let's have some questions on some other subject. [applause from audience]

Amy Goodman: Dr Kissinger, you said that the United States has won everything it wanted in the Cold War up to this point. I wanted to go back to the issue of Indonesia and before there's a booing in the audience, just to say as you talk about China and India, Indonesia is the fourth largest country in the world. And so I wanted to ask the question in a current way about East Timor. And that is, given what has happened in the twenty years, the 200,000 people who have been killed, according to Amnesty, according to Asia Watch, even according to the Indonesian military. . . . Do you see that as a success of the United States?

Kissinger: No, but I don't think it's an American policy. We cannot be, we're not responsible for everything that happens in every place in the world. [applause from audience]

Goodman: Except that 90 percent of the weapons used during the invasion were from the US and it continues to this day. So in that way we are intimately connected to Indonesia, unfortunately. Given that, I was wondering if you think it's a success and whether too, with you on the board of Freeport McMoRan, which has the largest gold-mining operation in the world in Indonesia, in Irian Jaya, are you putting pressure, since Freeport is such a major lobbyist in Congress on behalf of Indonesia, to change that policy and to support self-determination for the people of East Timor?

Kissinger: The, uh, the United States as a general proposition cannot fix every problem on the use of American weapons in purely civil conflicts. We should do our best to prevent this. As a private American corporation engaged in private business in an area far removed from Timor but in Indonesia, I do not believe it is their job to get itself involved in that issue because if they do, then no American private enterprise will be welcome there anymore.

Goodman: But they do every day, and lobby Congress.

It is interesting to notice, in that final answer, the final decomposition of Kissinger's normally efficient if robotic syntax. (For more material on his involvement with Freeport McMoRan, and his other holdings in a privatized military–political–commercial complex, see Chapter 10.) It's also fascinating to see, once again, the operations of his denial mechanism. If Kissinger and his patron Nixon were identified with any one core belief, it was that the United States should never be, or even appear to be, a "pitiful, helpless giant." Kissinger's own writings and speeches are heavily larded with rhetoric about "credibility" and the need to impress friend and foe with the mettle of American resolve. Yet, in response to any inquiry that might implicate him in crime and fiasco, he rushes to humiliate his own country and its professional servants, suggesting that they know little, care less, are poorly informed and easily rattled by the pace of events. He also resorts to a demagogic isolationism. In "signaling" terms, this is as much as to claim that the United States is a pushover for any ambitious or irredentist banana republic.

This semi-conscious reversal of rhetoric also leads to renewed episodes of hysterical and improvised lying. (Recall his claim to the Chinese that it was the Soviet Union that had instigated the Turkish invasion of Cyprus.) The idea that Indonesia's annexation of Timor may be compared to India's occupation of Goa is too absurd to have been cited in any apologia before or since. What Kissinger seems to like about the comparison is the rapidity with which Goa was forgotten. What he overlooks is that it was forgotten because (1) it was not a bloodbath and (2) it completed the decolonization of India. The Timor bloodbath represented the *cementing* of colonization by Indonesia. And clearly, an Indonesian invasion that began a few hours after Kissinger had stepped off the tarmac at Jakarta airport must have been planned and readied several days before he arrived. Such plans would have been known by any embassy military attaché worth the name, and certainly by any visiting secretary of state. We have the word of C. Philip Liechty, a former CIA operations officer in Indonesia, that:

> Suharto was given the green light to do what he did. There was discussion in the Embassy and in traffic with the State Department about the problems that would be created for us if the public and Congress became aware of the level and type of military assistance that was going to Indonesia at that time. Without continued heavy US military support the Indonesians might not have been able to pull it off.

Given that legal and international responsibility for East Timor rested with Portugal, a long-term NATO ally of the United States, the decision to disregard this, and at the admitted minimum to say nothing to the Indonesians about it, must have been deliberate. Given Kissinger's acute preoccupation with the fate of the Portuguese empire – as we will see – it may have been even more than that. It certainly cannot have been the result of inattention, or of the pressure of other distracting world events in (to take Kissinger's own cited instance) the other Portuguese colony of Angola.

The desire to appear to have been uninvolved may – if we are charitable – have arisen in part from the fact that even Indonesia's Foreign Minister, Adam Malik, conceded in public a death toll of between 50,000 and 80,000 Timorese civilians in the first eighteen months of Indonesia's war of subjugation (in other words on Kissinger's watch) and inflicted with weapons that he bent American laws to furnish to the killers. Now that a form of democracy has returned to Indonesia, which in its first post-dictatorial act renounced the annexation and – after a bloody last pogrom by its auxiliaries – withdrew from the territory, we may be able to learn more exactly the extent of the genocide.

Kissinger's surreptitious conduct is made very plain by the State Department cable of December 1975, and the subsequent memorandum concerning it. In point of fact, the essential decisions about Portugal's ex-colonies had been made during the preceding July, when Kissinger had secured presidential permission for a covert program of military intervention, coordinated with the South Africans and General Mobutu, to impose a tribalist regime upon Angola. The following month, as a matter of record, he informed the Indonesian generals that he would not oppose their intervention in East Timor. The only bargaining in December involved a request that Indonesia delay the start of its own colonial adventure until after Air Force One, carrying Ford and Kissinger, had left Indonesian airspace.

This "deniable" pattern did not dispose of two matters of legality, both of them in the province of the State Department. The first was the violation of international law by Indonesia, in a case where jurisdiction clearly rested with a Portuguese and NATO government of which Kissinger (partly as a result of its support for "decolonization") did not approve. The second was the violation of American law, which stipulated that weapons supplied to Indonesia were to be employed only for self-defense. State Department officials, bound by law, were likewise bound to conclude that United States aid to the generals in Jakarta would have to be cut off. Their memo summarizing this case was the cause of the tremendous internal row that is minuted below, in a declassified State Department transcript:

SECRET/SENSITIVE

MEMORANDUM OF CONVERSATION

Participants: The Secretary [Henry Kissinger]
Deputy Secretary [Robert] Ingersoll
Under Secretary [for Political Affairs Joseph] Sisco
Under Secretary [Carlyle] Maw
Deputy Under Secretary [Lawrence] Eagleburger
Assistant Secretary [Philip] Habib
Monroe Leigh, Legal Advisor
Jerry Bremer, Notetaker
Date: December 18, 1975
Subject: Department Policy

The Secretary [Kissinger]: I want to raise a little bit of hell about the Department's conduct in my absence. Until last week I thought we had a disciplined group; now we've gone to pieces completely. Take this cable on [East] Timor. You know my mind and attitude and anyone who knows my position as you do must know that I would not have approved it. The only consequence is to put yourself on record. It is a disgrace to treat the Secretary of State this way. . . .

What possible explanation is there for it? I had told you to stop it quietly. What is your place doing, Phil, to let this happen? It is incomprehensible. It is wrong in substance and procedure. It is a disgrace. Were you here?
Habib: No.

. . .

Habib: Our assessment was that if it was going to be trouble, it would come up before your return. And I was told they decided it was desirable to go ahead with the cable.

[*Kissinger*]: Nonsense. I said do it for a few weeks and then open up again.

Habib: The cable will not leak.

[*Kissinger*]: Yes it will and it will go to Congress too and then we will have hearings on it.

Habib: I was away. I was told by cable that it had come up.

[*Kissinger*]: That means that there are two cables! And that means twenty guys have seen it.

Habib: No, I got it back-channel – it was just one paragraph double talk and cryptic so I knew what it was talking about. I was told that Leigh thought that there was a legal requirement to do it.

Leigh: No, I said it could be done administratively. It was not in our interest to do it on legal grounds.

Sisco: We were told that you had decided we had to stop.

[*Kissinger*]: Just a minute, just a minute. You all know my view on this. You must have an FSO-8 [Foreign Service Officer, Class Eight] who knows it well. It will have a devastating impact on Indonesia. There's this masochism in the extreme here. No one has complained that it was aggression.

Leigh: The Indonesians were violating an agreement with us.

[*Kissinger*]: The Israelis when they go into Lebanon – when was the last time we protested that?

Leigh: That's a different situation.

Maw: It is self-defense.

[*Kissinger*]: And we can't construe a Communist government in the middle of Indonesia as self-defense?

Leigh: Well . . .

[*Kissinger*]: Then you're saying that arms can't be used for defense?

Habib: No, they can be used for the defense of Indonesia.

[*Kissinger*]: Now take a look at this basic theme that is coming out on Angola. These SOBs are leaking all of this stuff to [*New York Times* reporter] Les Gelb.

Sisco: I can tell you who.

[*Kissinger*]: Who?

Sisco: [National Security Council member William] Hyland spoke to him.

[*Kissinger*]: Wait a minute – Hyland said . . .

Sisco: He said he briefed Gelb.

[*Kissinger*]: I want these people to know that our concern in Angola is not the economic wealth or a naval base. It has to do with the USSR operating 8,000 miles from home when all the surrounding states are asking for our help. This will affect the Europeans, the Soviets, and China.

On the Timor thing, that will leak in three months, and *it will come out that Kissinger overruled his pristine bureaucrats and violated the law.* How many people in L [the legal advisor's office] know about this? [italics added]

Leigh: Three.

Habib: There are at least two in my office.

[*Kissinger*]: Plus everybody in the meeting so you're talking about not less than 15 or 20. You have a responsibility to recognize that we are living in a revolutionary situation. Everything on paper will be used against me.

Habib: We do that and take account of that all the time.

. . .

[*Kissinger*]: Every day some SOB in the Department is carrying on about Angola but no one is defending Angola. Find me one quote in the Gelb article defending our policy in Angola.

Habib: I think the leaks and dissent are the burden you have to bear.

[*Kissinger*]: But the people in charge of this Department could have lacerated AF [Bureau for African Affairs].

Ingersoll: I was told it came from up the river.

Eagleburger: No way.

[*Kissinger*]: Don't be ridiculous. It's quoted there. Read Gelb. Was [Assistant Secretary of State for African Affairs William] Schaufele called in and told to get his house under control? This is not minor league stuff. We are going to lose big. The President says to the Chinese that we're going to stand firm in Angola and two weeks later we get out. I go to a NATO meeting and meanwhile the Department leaks that we're worried about a naval base and says it's an exaggeration or aberration of Kissinger's. I don't care about the oil or the base but I do care about the African reaction when they see the Soviets pull it off and we don't do anything. If the Europeans then say to themselves if they can't hold Luanda, how can they defend Europe? The Chinese will say we're a country that was run out of Indochina for 50,000 men and is now being run out of Angola for less than $50m. Where were the meetings here yesterday. Were there any?

. . .

[*Kissinger*]: It cannot be that our agreement with Indonesia says that the arms are for internal purposes only. I think you will find that it says that they are legitimately used for self-defense.

There are two problems. The merits of the case which you had a duty to raise with me. The second is how to put these to me. But to put it into a cable 30 hours before I return, knowing how cables are handled in this building, guarantees that it will be a national disaster and that transcends whatever [Deputy Legal Advisor George] Aldrich has in his feverish mind.

I took care of it with the administrative thing by ordering Carlyle [Maw] not to make any new sales. How will the situation get better in six weeks?

Habib: They may get it cleaned up by then.

[*Kissinger*]: The Department is falling apart and has reached the point where it disobeys clear-cut orders.

Habib: We sent the cable because we thought it was needed and we thought it needed your attention. This was ten days ago.

[*Kissinger*]: Nonsense. When did I get the cable, Jerry?

Bremer: Not before the weekend. I think perhaps on Sunday.

[*Kissinger*]: You had to know what my view on this was. *No one who has worked with me in the last two years could not know what my view would be on Timor.* [italics added]

Habib: Well, let us look at it – talk to Leigh. There are still some legal requirements. I can't understand why it went out if it was not legally required.

[*Kissinger*]: Am I wrong in assuming that the Indonesians will go up in smoke if they hear about this?

Habib: Well, it's better than a cutoff. It could be done at a low level.

[*Kissinger*]: We have four weeks before Congress comes back. That's plenty of time.

Leigh: The way to handle the administrative cutoff would be that we are studying the situation.

[*Kissinger*]: And 36 hours was going to be a major problem?

Leigh: We had a meeting in Sisco's office and decided to send the message.

[*Kissinger*]: I know what the law is but how can it be in the US national interest for us to give up on Angola and kick the Indonesians in the teeth? Once it is on paper, there will be a lot of FSO-6s who can make themselves feel good who can write for the Open Forum Panel on the thing even though I will turn out to be right in the end.

Habib: The second problem on leaking of cables is different.

[*Kissinger*]: No it's an empirical fact.

Eagleburger: Phil, it's a fact. You can't say that any NODIS ["No Distribution": most restricted level of classification] cable will leak but you can't count on three to six months later someone asking for it [*sic*] in Congress. If it's part of the written record, it will be dragged out eventually.

[*Kissinger*]: You have an obligation to the national interest. I don't care if we sell equipment to Indonesia or not. I get nothing from it, I get no rakeoff. But you have an obligation to figure out how to serve your country. The Foreign Service is not to serve itself. The Service stands for service to the United States and not service to the Foreign Service.

Habib: I understand that that's what this cable would do.

[*Kissinger*]: The minute you put this into the system you cannot resolve it without a finding.

Leigh: There's only one question. What do we say to Congress if we're asked?

[*Kissinger*]: We cut it off while we are studying it. We intend to start again in January.

The delivery of heavy weapons for use against civilian objectives did indeed resume in January 1976, after a short interval in which Congress was misled as advertised. Nobody, it must be said, comes especially well out of this meeting; the Secretary's civil servants were anything but "pristine." Still it can be noted of Kissinger that, in complete contrast to his public statements, he:

1. Forebore from any mention of Goa.
2. Did not trouble to conceal his long-held views on the matter, berating his underlings for being so dense as not to know them.
3. Did not affect to be taken by surprise by events in East Timor.
4. Admitted that he was breaking the law.
5. Felt it necessary to deny that he could profit personally from the arms shipments, a denial for which nobody had asked him.

Evidently, there was a dialectic in Kissinger's mind between Angola and East Timor, both of them many miles from US or Russian borders but both seen as tests of his own dignity. (The "surrounding states" to which he alludes in the Angolan case were apartheid South Africa and General

Mobutu's Zaire: the majority of African states, as a matter of record, opposed his intervention on the side of the tribalist and pro-South Africa militias in Angola. His favored regimes have long since collapsed in ignominy; the United States now recognizes the MPLA, with all its deformities, as the legitimate government of Angola. And of course, no European ever felt that the fate of the West hinged on Kissinger's gamble in Luanda.)

That Kissinger understood Portugal's continuing legal sovereignty in East Timor is shown by a NODIS memorandum of a Camp David meeting between himself, General Suharto and President Ford on the preceding 5 July 1975. Almost every line of the text has been deleted by official redaction, and much of the discussion is unilluminating except about the eagerness of the administration to supply naval, air and military equipment to the junta, but at one point, just before Kissinger makes his entrance, President Ford asks his guest, "Have the Portuguese set a date yet for allowing the Timor people to make their choice?" The entire answer is obliterated by deletion, but let it never be said that Kissinger's State Department did not know that Portugal was entitled, indeed mandated, to hold a free election for the Timorese. It is improbable that Suharto, in the excised answer, was assuring his hosts that such an open election would be won by candidates favoring annexation by Indonesia.

On 9 November 1979, Jack Anderson's column in the *Washington Post* published an interview on East Timor with ex-President Ford, and a number of classified US intelligence documents relating to the 1975 aggression. One of the latter papers describes how Indonesia's generals were pressing Suharto "to authorize direct military intervention," while another informs Messrs Ford and Kissinger that Suharto would raise the East Timor issue at their December 1975 meeting and would "try and elicit a sympathetic attitude." The relatively guileless Ford was happy to tell Anderson that the United States national interest "had to be on the side of Indonesia." He may or may not have been aware that he was thereby giving the lie to everything ever said by Kissinger on the subject.

9

A "WET JOB" IN WASHINGTON?

AS WE HAVE more than once seen, Kissinger has a tendency to personalize his politics. His policies have led directly and deliberately to the deaths of anonymous hundreds of thousands, but have also involved the targeting of certain inconvenient individuals – General Schneider, Archbishop Makarios, Sheik Mujib. And, as we have also more than once glimpsed, Kissinger has an especial relish for the Washington vendetta and the localized revenge.

It seems possible that these two tendencies converge in a single case: a plan to kidnap and murder a man named Elias P. Demetracopoulos. Mr Demetracopoulos is a distinguished Greek journalist with an unexampled record of opposition to the dictatorship that disfigured his homeland between 1967 and 1974. In the course of those years, he made his home in Washington, supporting himself as a consultant to a respected Wall Street firm. Innumerable senators, congressmen, Hill staffers, diplomats and reporters have testified to the extraordinary one-man campaign of lobbying and information he waged against the military gangsters who had usurped power in Athens. Since that same junta enjoyed the sympathy of powerful interests in Washington, Demetracopoulos was compelled to combat on two fronts, and made (as will shortly appear) some influential enemies.

After the collapse of the Greek dictatorship in 1974 – a collapse occasioned by the events I discuss in Chapter 7 on Cyprus above – Demetracopoulos gained access to the secret police files in Athens, and confirmed what he had long suspected. There had been more than one attempt made to kidnap and eliminate him. Files held by the KYP – the Greek equivalent of the CIA – revealed that the then dictator, George Papadopoulos, and his deputy security chief Michael Roufogalis several times contacted the Greek military mission in Washington with precisely this end in view. Stamped with the words "COSMIC: Eyes Only" – the highest security classification – this traffic involved a plethora of schemes. They had in common, it is of interest to note, a desire to see Demetracopoulos snatched from Washington and repatriated. An assassination in Washington might have been embarrassing; moreover there seems to have been a need to interrogate Demetracopoulos before despatching him. (The Greek junta was in 1970 expelled by the Council of Europe for its systematic use of torture against political opponents, and a series of public trials held in Athens after 1974 committed the torturers and their political masters to long terms of imprisonment.) One proposal was to smuggle Demetracopoulos aboard a Greek civilian airliner, another was to put him on a Greek military plane, and still another was to get him aboard a submarine. (If it were not for the proven record of irrationality and mania among the leaders of the junta, one might be tempted to dismiss at least the third of these plans as a fantasy.) One sentence stands out from the COSMIC cables:

> We can rely on the cooperation of the various agencies of the U.S. Government, but estimate the Congressional reaction to be fierce.

This was a sober estimate: the CIA and the NSC in particular were notoriously friendly to the junta, while Demetracopoulos enjoyed the benefit of many friendships among senators and members of the House.

Seeking to discover what kind of "cooperation" US agencies might have offered, Demetracopoulos in 1976 engaged an attorney – William A.

Dobrovir of the DC firm of Dobrovir, Oakes and Gebhardt – and brought suit under the Freedom of Information Act and the Privacy Act. He was able to obtain many hundreds of documents from the FBI, the CIA and the State Department, as well as the Department of Justice and the Pentagon. A number of these papers indicated that copies had been furnished to the National Security Council, then the domain of Henry Kissinger. But requests for documentation from this source were unavailing. As previously noted, Kissinger had on leaving office made a hostage of his own papers – copying them, classifying them as "personal," and deeding them to the Library of Congress on condition that they be held privately. Thus, Demetracopoulos met with a stone wall when he used the law to try and prise anything from the NSC. In March 1977, however, the NSC finally responded to repeated legal initiatives by releasing the skeletal "computer indices" of the files that had been kept on Demetracopoulos. Paging through these, his attention was not unnaturally caught by the following:

7024513 DOCUMENT= 5 OF 5 PAGE = 1 OF 1
KEYWORDS ACKNOWLEDGING SENS MOSS BURDICK GRAVEL RE MR DEMETRACOPOULOS
DEATH IN ATHENS PRISON DATE 701218

"Well it's not every day," said Demetracopoulos when I interviewed him, "that you read about your own death in a state document." His attorney was bound to agree, and wrote a series of letters to Kissinger asking for copies of the file to which the indices referred. For seven years – I repeat, for seven years – Kissinger declined to favor Demetracopoulos's lawyer with a reply. When he eventually did respond, it was only through his own lawyer, who wrote that:

Efforts were made to search the collection for copies of documents which meet the description provided. . . . No such copies could be found.

"Efforts were made" is, of course, a piece of obfuscation that might describe the most perfunctory inquiry. We are therefore left with the question: Did

Kissinger know of, or approve, or form a part of, that "cooperation of the various agencies of the U.S. Government" on which foreign despots had been counting for a design of kidnap, torture and execution?

To begin with an obvious question: Why should a figure of Kissinger's stature either know about, or care about, the existence of a lone dissident journalist? This question is easily answered: the record shows that Kissinger knew very well who Demetracopoulos was, and detested him into the bargain. The two men had actually met in Athens in 1956, when Demetracopoulos had hosted a luncheon at the Grande Bretagne Hotel for the visiting professor. Over the next decade, Demetracopoulos had been prominent among those warning of, and resisting, a military intervention in Greek politics. The CIA generally favored such an intervention and maintained intimate connections with those who were planning it: in November 1963 the director of the CIA, John McCone, signed an internal message asking for "any substantive derogatory data which can be used to deny [Dematracopoulos] subsequent entry to the US." No such derogatory information was in fact available, so that when the coup came, Demetracopoulos was able to settle in Washington, DC, and begin his exile campaign.

He began it auspiciously enough, by supplying "derogatory data" about the Nixon and Agnew campaign of 1968. This campaign – already tainted badly enough by the betrayal of the Vietnam peace negotiations – was also receiving illegal donations from the Greek military dictatorship.

The money came from Michael Roufogalis at the KYP and was handed over, in cash, to John Mitchell by an ultra-conservative Greek-American businessman named Thomas Pappas. The sum involved was $549,000 – a considerable amount by the standards of the day. Its receipt was doubly illegal: foreign governments are prohibited from making campaign donations (as are foreigners in general), and given that the KYP was in receipt of CIA subsidies there existed the further danger that American intelligence money was being recycled back into the American political process – in direct violation of the CIA's own charter.

In 1968, Demetracopoulos took his findings to Larry O'Brien, chairman of the Democratic National Committee, who issued a call for an inquiry into the activities of Pappas and the warm relations existing between the Nixon–Agnew campaign and the Athens junta. A number of historians have since speculated as to whether it was evidence for this "Greek connection," with its immense potential for damage, that Nixon's and Mitchell's burglars were seeking when they entered O'Brien's Watergate office under the cover of night. Considerable weight is lent to this view by one salient fact: when the Nixon White House was seeking "hush money" for the burglars, it turned to Thomas Pappas to provide it.

Demetracopoulos's dangerous knowledge of the secret campaign donations, and his incessant lobbying on the Hill and in the press against Nixon's and Kissinger's client regime in Athens, drew unwelcome attention to him. He later sued both the FBI and the CIA – becoming the first person ever to do so successfully – and received written admissions from both agencies that they possessed "no derogatory information" about him. In the course of these suits, he also secured an admission from then FBI director William Webster that he had been under "rather extensive" surveillance on and between the following dates: 9 November 1967 and 2 October 1969; 25 August 1971 and 14 March 1973; and 19 February and 24 October 1974.

Unaware of the precise extent of this surveillance, Demetracopoulos had nonetheless more than once found himself brushed by a heavy hand. On 7 September 1971 he was lunching at Washington's fashionable Jockey Club with Nixon's chief henchman, Murray Chotiner, who told him bluntly, "Lay off Pappas. You can be in trouble. You can be deported. It's not smart politics. You know Tom Pappas is a friend of the President." The next month, on 27 October 1971, Demetracopoulos was lunching with columnist Robert Novak at the Sans Souci and was threatened by Pappas himself, who came over from an adjacent table to tell him and Novak that he could make trouble for anyone who wanted him investigated. On the preceding 12 July, Demetracopoulos had testified before the European subcommittee of the House Foreign Affairs Committee, chaired by Congressman Benjamin Rosenthal of New York, about the influence of Thomas Pappas on US foreign policy and the Athens dictatorship (and vice versa). Before his oral testimony could be printed, a Justice Department agent appeared at the subcommittee's office and demanded a copy of the statement. Demetracopoulos had then, on 17 September, furnished a memorandum on Pappas's activities to the same subcommittee. His written deposition closed thus: "Finally, I have submitted separately to the subcommittee items of documentary evidence which I believe will be useful." This statement, wrote Rowland Evans and Robert Novak in their syndicated column, caused "extreme nervousness in the Nixon White House."

Later disclosures have accustomed us to the part-mafioso and part-banana-republic atmosphere in Washington during those years; it was still very shocking for Demetracopoulos to receive a letter from Ms Louise Gore. Ms Gore has since become more celebrated as the cousin of Vice-President Albert Gore and the proprietress of the Fairfax Hotel in Washington, DC, where the boy politician grew up. She was then quite celebrated in her own right: as a Republican state Senator from Maryland, and as the woman who introduced Spiro Agnew to Richard Nixon. She was a close friend of Attorney General Mitchell, and had been appointed as Nixon's representative to UNESCO. Demetracopoulos lived, along with many congressmen and political types, as a tenant of an apartment in her hotel. He had also been a friend of hers since 1959. On 24 January 1972 she wrote to him:

> Dear Elias –
> I went to Perle's [Perle Mesta's] luncheon for Martha Mitchell yesterday and sat next to John. He is *furious* at you – and your testimony against Pappas. He kept threatening to have you deported!!
>
> At first I tried to ask him if he had any reason to think you could be deported and he didn't have any answer – But then tried to counter by asking me what I knew about you and why we were friends.
>
> It really got out of hand. It was all he'd talk about during lunch and everyone at the table was listening . . .

Among those present at the table were George Bush, then ambassador to the United Nations, and numerous other diplomats. The Attorney

General's lack of restraint and want of tact, on such an occasion and at the very table of legendary hostess Perle Mesta, were clearly symptomatic of a considerable irritation, even rage.

I have related this background in order to show that Demetracopoulos was under surveillance, that he possessed information highly damaging to an important Nixon–Kissinger client regime, and that his identity was well known to those in power, in both Washington and Athens. The United States ambassador in Athens at the time was Henry Tasca, a Nixon and Kissinger crony with a very lenient attitude to the dictatorship. (He later testified to a closed session of Congress that he had known of the 1968 payments by the Greek secret police to the Nixon campaign.) In July 1971, shortly after Demetracopoulos testified before Congressman Rosenthal's subcommittee, Tasca had sent a four-page secret cable from Athens. It began:

> For some time I have felt that Elias Demetracopoulos is head of a well-organized conspiracy which deserves serious investigation. We have seen how effective he has been in combatting our present policy in Greece. His aim is to damage our relations with Greece, loosen our NATO alliance and weaken the U.S. security position in the Eastern Mediterranean.

This was certainly taking Demetracopoulos seriously. So was the closing paragraph, which read as follows:

> I am therefore bringing the matter to your personal attention in the hope that a way will be found to step up an investigation of Demetracopoulos to identify his sponsors, his sources of funds, his intentions, his methods of work and his fellow conspirators. . . . I bring this matter to your attention now, believing that as an alien resident in the United States it may be possible to submit him to the kind of searching and professional FBI investigation which would lift some of the mystery.

The cable was addressed, as is usual from an ambassador, to Secretary of State William Rogers. Yet it was also addressed – highly unusually – to Attorney General John Mitchell. But Mitchell, as we have seen, was the only attorney general ever to serve on Henry Kissinger's supervisory Forty Committee, which oversaw covert operations.

The State Department duly urged that "the Department of Justice do everything possible to see if we can make a Foreign Agent's case, or any kind of a case for that matter" against Demetracopoulos. Of course, as was later admitted, these investigations turned up nothing. The influence wielded by Demetracopoulos did not derive from any sinister source or nexus. But when he said that the Greek dictatorship had trampled its own society, used censorship and torture, threatened Cyprus, and bought itself political influence in Washington, he was uttering potent factual truths. Nixon himself confirmed the connection, between the junta and Pappas and Tasca and the two-way flow of dirty money, on a post-Watergate White House tape dated 23 May 1973. He is talking to his renowned confidential secretary, Rose Mary Woods:

> Good old Tom Pappas, as you probably know or heard, if you haven't already heard, it is true, helped, at Mitchell's request, fund-raising for some of the defendants. . . . He came up to see me on March 7, Pappas did. Pappas came to see me about the ambassador to Greece, that he wanted to – he wanted to keep Henry Tasca there.

This same dictatorship had in June 1970 revoked Demetracopoulos's Greek citizenship, so he was a stateless person travelling only on a flimsy document giving him leave to re-enter the United States. This fact assumed its own importance in December 1970, when his blind father was dying of pneumonia, alone, in Athens. Demetracopoulos sought permission to return home under a safe-conduct or *laissez-passer*, and was able to enlist numerous congressional friends in the attempt. Among them were senators Frank E. Moss of Utah, Quentin N. Burdick of North Dakota, and Mike Gravel of Alaska, who signed a letter dated 11 December to the Greek government and to Ambassador Tasca. Senators Edward Kennedy of Massachusetts and William Fulbright of Arkansas also expressed a personal interest.

Neither the Athens regime nor Tasca replied directly, but on 20 December, four days after the old man had died without a visit from his only son, Senators Moss, Burdick, and Gravel received a telegram from the Greek embassy in Washington. This instructed them that Demetracopoulos should have applied in person to the embassy: an odd demand to make of a man whose passport and citizenship had just been cancelled by the dictatorship. Meanwhile, Demetracopoulos received a telephone call at his home, from Senator Kennedy in person, advising him not to accept any safe-conduct offer from Greece even if he was offered it. Had Demetracopoulos presented himself at the junta's embassy, he might well have been detained and kidnapped, in accordance with one of the plans we now know had been readied for his "disappearance." Of course, such a scheme would have been extremely difficult to carry out in the absence of some "cooperation" – at least a blind eye – from local US intelligence officials.

Declassified cable traffic between Ambassador Tasca in Athens and Kissinger's deputy Joseph Sisco at the State Department shows that Senator Kennedy's misgivings were amply justified. In a cable dated 14 December from Sisco to Tasca, the ambassador was told: "If GOG [Government of Greece] permits Demetracopoulos to enter, quite clearly we must avoid being put in a position of guaranteeing any assurances that he may have of being able to depart." Concurring with this extraordinary statement, Tasca added that there was a possibility of Senator Gravel attending the funeral of Demetracopoulos senior. Elias, wrote the ambassador, "undoubtedly hopes to exploit Senator's visit by providing some way of proving that conditions here are as repressive as he has been representing them to be. He could even try to arrange for some manifestation of violence, such as a small bomb."

The absurdity of this – Demetracopoulos had no record whatever of the advocacy or practice of violence, as Tasca subconsciously recognized by making the hypothetical bomb a "small" one – also has its sinister side. Suggested here is just the sort of alibi or provocation or pretext that the junta might need for a frame-up, or to cover up a "disappearance." The entire correspondence reeks of the unspoken priorities of both the embassy and the State Department, which reflect their contempt for elected United States senators, their dislike of dissent, and their need to gratify a group of Greek gangsters who are now rightly serving terms of life imprisonment.

Now look again at the computer index disgorged, after years of litigation, from Kissinger's NSC files. It bears the date of 18 December 1970 and appears to apprise Senators Moss, Burdick and Gravel that Demetracopoulos had met his end in an Athens prison. Was this a contingency plan? A cover story? As long as Dr Kissinger maintains his stubborn silence, and the control over his "private" state papers, it will be impossible to determine.

The same applies to the second attempt on Mr Demetracopoulos of which we have knowledge. Having avoided the trap that seems to have been set for him in 1970, Demetracopoulos kept up his fusillade of leaks and disclosures, aimed at discrediting the Greek junta and embarrassing its American friends. He also became an important voice warning of the junta's designs on the independence of Cyprus and of US indifference to (or complicity in) that policy. In this capacity (discussed in detail in Chapter 7) he became a source of annoyance to Henry Kissinger. This can be established without difficulty. In a briefing paper presented to President Gerald Ford in October 1974, there are references to a "trace paper" about Demetracopoulos, to "the derogatory blind memo" about him, and to "the long Kissinger memo" on him. Once again, and despite repeated requests from lawyers, Kissinger has declined to answer any queries about the whereabouts of these papers, or shed any light on their contents. However, his National Security Council asked the FBI to amass any information that might discredit Demetracopoulos, and between 1972 and 1974, according to papers since declassified, the Bureau furnished Kissinger with slanderous and false material concerning, among other things, a romance which Demetracopoulos was allegedly conducting with a woman now dead, and a supposed relationship between him and Daniel Ellsberg, leaker of the celebrated "Pentagon Papers," a man he has never met.

This might seem trivial, were it not for the memoirs of Constantine Panayotakos, the ambassador of the Greek junta to Washington, DC.

Arriving to take up his post in February 1974, as the ambassador wrote in his later memoirs, entitled *In the First Line of Defense*:

> I was informed about some plans to kidnap and transport Elias Demetracopoulos to Greece; plans which reminded me of KGB methods.... On 29 May a document was transmitted to me from Angelos Vlachos, Secretary General of the Foreign Ministry, giving the views of the United States ambassador Henry Tasca, which he agreed with, about the most efficient means of dealing with the conspiracies and the whole activity of Demetracopoulos. Tasca's views are included in a memorandum of conversation with the Foreign Minister Spyridon Tetenes of 27 May.
>
> Finally, another brilliant idea of the most brilliant members of the Foreign Ministry in Athens, transmitted to me on 12 June, was for me to seek useful advice on the *extermination* of Elias Demetracopoulos from George Churchill, director of the Greek desk at the State Department, who was one of his most vitriolic enemies. [italics added]

(In Greek, the italicized word above is *exoudeterosi*. It is pretty strong. It is usually translated as "extermination," though "elimination" might be an alternative rendering. It is not a recipe for inconveniencing or hampering an individual, but for getting rid of him.) Ambassador Panayotakos later wrote a detailed letter, which is in my possession, that he had direct knowledge of a plan to abduct Demetracopoulos from Washington. His testimony is corroborated by an affidavit which I also possess, signed under penalty of perjury by Charalambos Papadopoulos. Papadopoulos was at the time the Political Counsellor to the Greek embassy – the number three position – and was bidden to lunch at the nearby Jockey Club, in late May or early June of 1974, by Ambassador Panayotakos and the assistant military attaché, Lieutenant Colonel Sotiris Yiounis. At the lunch, Yiounis broached the question of the kidnapping of Demetracopoulos, who was to be smuggled aboard a Greek NATO submarine at a harbor in Virginia.

Papadopoulos, who was Greek ambassador to Pakistan at the time he swore his affidavit, has since said that he was assured that Henry Kissinger was fully aware of the proposed operation, and "most probably willing to act as its umbrella." By that stage, the Greek junta had only a few weeks to live because of its crimes in Cyprus. Since the fall of the dictatorship, even more extensive evidence of the junta's assassination plans has been uncovered, if only at the Athenian end of the plot. But this was not a regime which ever acted without Washington's "understanding." Attempts to unearth more detail have also been made in Washington. In 1975 senators George McGovern and James Abourezk, seconded by Congressman Don Edwards of the House Intelligence Committee, asked Senator Frank Church to include the kidnap plot against Demetracopoulos in the investigative work of his famous committee on US intelligence. As first reported by the *New York Times* and then confirmed by Seymour Hersh, Kissinger intervened personally with Church, citing grave but unspecified matters of national security, to have this aspect of the investigation shut down.

Some of this may seem fantastic, but we do know that Kissinger was conducting a vendetta against Demetracopoulos (as was Ambassador Henry Tasca); we do know that Kissinger was involved in high-level collusion with the Greek junta and had advance knowledge of the plot to assassinate Archbishop Makarios; and we do know that he had used the US embassy in Chile to smuggle weapons for the contract killing of General René Schneider. The cover story in that case, too, was that the hired goons were "only" trying to kidnap him . . .

We also know that two clients of Kissinger's Forty Committee, General Pinochet and Colonel Manuel Contreras, made use of the Chilean embassy in Washington to murder the dissident leader Orlando Letelier, not long after being received and flattered and in one case paid by Kissinger and his surrogates.

Thus the Demetracopoulos story, told here in full for the first time, makes a *prima facie* case that Henry Kissinger was at least aware of a plan to abduct and interrogate, and almost certainly kill, a civilian journalist in Washington, DC. In order to be cleared of the suspicion, and to explain the mysterious reference to Demetracopoulos's death in his own archives, Kissinger need only make those same archives at last accessible – or else be subpoenaed to do so.

10

AFTERWORD: THE PROFIT MARGIN

IN HIS FURIOUS meeting at the State Department on 18 December 1975, shortly after his moment of complicity with the Indonesian generals over East Timor (see pages 101–6), Kissinger makes the following peculiar disavowal:

> "I don't care if we sell equipment to Indonesia or not. I get nothing from it,
> I get no rakeoff."

One might have taken it for granted that a serving secretary of state had no direct interest in the sale of weapons to a foreign dictatorship; nobody at the meeting had suggested any such thing. How peculiar that Kissinger should deny an allegation that had not been made: answer a question that had not been asked.

It isn't possible to state with certainty when Kissinger began to profit personally from his association with the ruling circles in Indonesia, nor can it be definitely asserted that this profit was part of any "understanding" that originated in 1975. It's just that there is a perfect congruence between Kissinger's foreign policy counsel and his own business connections. One might call it a harmony of interests, rather than a conflict.

Six years after he left office, Kissinger set up a private consulting firm named Kissinger Associates, which exists to smooth and facilitate contact between multinational corporations and foreign governments. The client list is secret, and contracts with "the Associates" contain a clause prohibiting any mention of the arrangement, but corporate clients include or have included American Express, Shearson Lehmann, Arco, Daewoo of South Korea, H.J. Heinz, ITT Lockheed, Anheuser-Busch, the Banca Nazionale del Lavoro, Coca-Cola, Fiat, Revlon, Union Carbide, and the Midland Bank. Kissinger's initial fellow "associates" were General Brent Scowcroft and Lawrence Eagleburger, both of whom had worked closely with him in the foreign policy and national security branches of government.

Numerous instances of a harmony between this firm and Kissinger's policy pronouncements can be cited. The best-known is probably that of the People's Republic of China. Kissinger assisted several American conglomerates, notably H.J. Heinz, to gain access to the Chinese market. As it was glowingly phrased by Anthony J.F. O'Reilly, CEO of Heinz:

> Kissinger and his associates make a real contribution, and we think they are particularly helpful in countries with more centrally planned economies, where the principal players and the dynamics among the principal players are of critical importance. This is particularly true in China, where he is a popular figure and is viewed with particular respect. On China, basically, we were well on our way to establishing the baby food presence there before Henry got involved. But once we decided to move he had practical points to offer, such as on the relationship between Taiwan and Beijing. He was helpful in seeing that we did not take steps that would not have been helpful in Beijing. His relevance obviously varies from market to market, but he's probably at his best in helping with contacts in that shadowy world where that counts.

The Chinese term for this zone of shadowy transactions is *guan-xi*. In less judgmental American speech it would probably translate as "access," or influence-peddling. Selling baby food in China may seem innocuous enough, but when the Chinese regime turned its guns and tanks on its own children in Tienanmen Square in 1989, it had no more staunch defender than Henry Kissinger. Arguing very strongly against sanctions, he wrote that "China remains too important for America's national security to risk the relationship on the emotions of the moment." Taking the Deng Xiaoping view of the democratic turbulence, and even the view of those we now suppose to have pressed Deng from the Right, he added, "No government in the world would have tolerated having the main square of its capital occupied for eight weeks by tens of thousands of demonstrators." Of course, some governments would have found a way to meet with the leaders of those demonstrators. . . . It is perhaps just as well that Kissinger's services were not retained by the Stalinist regimes of Romania, Czechoslovakia and East Germany, which succumbed to just such public insolence later in the same year.

Nor was Kissinger's influence-peddling confined to Heinz's nutritious products. He assisted Atlantic Richfield/Arco to market oil deposits in China. He helped ITT (a corporation which had once helped him to overthrow the elected government of Chile) to hold a path-breaking board meeting in Beijing, and he performed similar services for David Rockefeller and the Chase Manhattan Bank, which held an international advisory committee meeting in the Chinese capital and met with Deng himself.

Six months before the massacre in Tienanmen Square, Kissinger set up a limited investment partnership named China Ventures, of which he personally was chairman, CEO and chief partner. Its brochure helpfully explained that China Ventures involved itself only with projects that "enjoy the unquestioned support of the People's Republic of China." The move proved premature: the climate for investment on the Chinese mainland soured after the repression that followed the Tienanmen Square massacres, and the limited sanctions approved by Congress. This no doubt contributed to Kissinger's irritation at the criticism of Deng. But while China Ventures lasted, it drew large commitments from American Express, Coca-Cola, Heinz and a large mining and extraction conglomerate named Freeport McMoRan, of which more in a moment.

Many of Kissinger's most extreme acts have been undertaken, at least ostensibly, in the name of anti-Communism. So it is amusing to find him exerting himself on behalf of a regime that can guarantee safe investment by virtue of a ban on trade unions, a slave-labor prison system, and a one-party ideology. Nor is China the sole example here. When Lawrence Eagleburger left the State Department in 1984, having been ambassador to Yugoslavia, he became simultaneously a partner of Kissinger Associates, a director of a wholly owned banking subsidiary of the Ljubljanska Banka, a bank then owned by the Belgrade regime, and the American representative of the Yugo mini-car. Yugo duly became a client of Kissinger Associates, as did a Yugoslav construction concern named Enerjoprojeckt. The Yugo is of particular interest because it was produced by the large state-run conglomerate that also functioned as Yugoslavia's military–industrial and arms-manufacturing complex. This complex was later seized by Slobodan Milosevic, along with the other sinews of what had been the Yugoslav National Army, and used to prosecute wars of aggression against four neighboring republics. At all times during this protracted crisis, and somewhat out of step with many of his usually hawkish colleagues, Henry Kissinger urged a consistent policy of conciliation with the Milosevic regime. (Mr Eagleburger in due course rejoined the State Department as Deputy Secretary and briefly became Secretary of State. So it goes.)

Another instance of the Kissingerian practice is the dual involvement of "the Associates" with Saddam Hussein. When Saddam was riding high in the late 1980s, and having his way with the departments of Commerce and Agriculture in Washington, and throwing money around like the proverbial drunken sailor (and using poison gas and chemical weapons on his Kurdish population without a murmur from Washington), the US–Iraq Business Forum provided a veritable slot-machine of contacts, contracts and opportunities. Kissinger's partner Alan Stoga, who had also been the economist attached to his Reagan-era Commission on Central America, featured noticeably on a Forum junket to Baghdad. At the same time, Kissinger's firm represented the shady Italian Banco Nazionale del Lavoro, which was later shown to have made illegal loans to the Hussein regime. As usual, everything was legal. It always is, when the upper middle class meets the lower Middle East.

In the same year – 1989 – Kissinger made his lucrative connection with Freeport McMoRan, a globalized firm based in New Orleans. Its business is the old-fashioned one of extracting oil, gas, and minerals. Its chairman, James Moffett, has probably earned the favorite titles bestowed by the business and financial pages, being beyond any doubt "flamboyant," "buccaneering," and a "venture capitalist."

In 1989, Freeport McMoRan paid Kissinger Associates a retainer of $200,000 and fees of $600,000, not to mention a promise of a 2 percent commission on future earnings. Freeport McMoRan also made Kissinger a member of its board of directors, at an annual salary of at least $30,000. In 1990, the two concerns went into business in Burma, the most grimly repressive state in all of South Asia. Freeport McMoRan would drill for oil and gas, according to the agreement, and Kissinger's other client, Daewoo (which was then itself a venal corporate prop of an unscrupulous Korean regime), would build the plant. However, that year the Burmese generals, under their wonderful collective title of SLORC (State Law and Order Restoration Council), lost a popular election to the democratic opposition led by Daw Aung San Suu Kyi and decided to annul the result. This development – producing yet more irritating calls for the isolation of the Burmese junta – was unfavorable to the Kissinger– Freeport–Daewoo triad, and the proposal lapsed.

But the following year, in March 1991, Kissinger was back in Indonesia with Moffett, closing a deal for a thirty-year license to continue exploiting a gigantic gold and copper mine. The mine is of prime importance for three reasons. First, it was operated as part of a joint venture with the Indonesian military government, and with that government's leader, the now-deposed General Suharto. Second, it is located on the island of Irian Jaya (in an area formerly known as West Irian): a part of the archipelago which – in common with East Timor – is only Indonesian by right of arbitrary conquest. Third, its operations commenced in 1973 – two years before Henry Kissinger visited Indonesia and helped unleash the Indonesian bloodbath in East Timor while unlocking a flow of weaponry to his future business partners.

This could mean no more than the "harmony of interest" I suggested above. No more, in other words, than a happy coincidence. What is not coincidental is the following:

- Freeport McMoRan's enormous Grasberg mine in Irian Jaya stands accused of creating an environmental and social catastrophe. In October 1995 the Overseas Private Investment Corporation (OPIC), a Federal body that exists to help US companies overseas, decided to cancel Freeport McMoRan's investment insurance for political risk – the very element on which Kissinger had furnished soothing assurances in 1991. OPIC concluded that the Grasberg mine had "created and continues to pose unreasonable or major environmental, health or safety hazards with respect to the rivers that are being impacted by the tailings, the surrounding terrestrial ecosystem, and the local inhabitants."
- The "local inhabitants" who came last on that list are the Amungme people, whose protests at the environmental rape, and at working conditions in the mine, were met by Indonesian regular soldiers at the service of Freeport McMoRan, and under the orders of Suharto. In March 1996, large-scale rioting nearly closed the mine at a cost of four deaths and many injuries.

Freeport McMoRan mounted an intense lobbying campaign in Washington, with Kissinger's help, to get its OPIC insurance reinstated. The price was the creation of a trust fund of $100 million for the repair of the Grasberg site after it, and its surrounding ecology, had eventually been picked clean. All of this became moot with the overthrow of the Suharto dictatorship, the detention of Suharto himself, and the unmasking of an enormous nexus of "crony capitalism" involving him, his family, his military colleagues, and certain favored multinational corporations. This political revolution also restored, at incalculable human cost, the independence of East Timor. There was even a suggestion of a war crimes inquiry and a human rights tribunal, to settle some part of the account for the years of genocide and occupation. Once again, Henry Kissinger has had to scan the news with anxiety, and wonder whether even worse revelations are in store for him. It will be a national and international disgrace if the answer to this question is left to the pillaged and misgoverned people of Indonesia, rather than devolving onto a United States Congress that has for so long shirked its proper responsibility.

The subject awaits its magistrate.

11

LAW AND JUSTICE

ALTHOUGH ONE COULD do no more than "deplore" a number of slaughtered children, there was in existence means of preventing one particular aspect of the principle of expediency from doing too much damage. Most international criminals were beyond the reach of man-made laws; Dimitrios happened to be within reach of one law. He had committed at least two murders and had therefore broken the law as surely as if he had been starving and had stolen a loaf of bread.

Eric Ambler, *The Mask of Dimitrios*

As Henry Kissinger now understands, there are increasingly noticeable rents and tears in the cloak of immunity that has shrouded him until now. Recent evolutions in national and international law have made his position an exposed and, indeed, a vulnerable one. For convenience, the distinct areas of law may be grouped under four main headings:

1. International Human Rights Law. This comprises the grand and sonorous covenants on the rights of the individual in relation to the state; it also protects the individual from other actors in the international community who might violate those rights. Following from the French Revolution's "Declaration of the Rights of Man," international human-rights law holds that political associations are legitimate only

insofar as they preserve the dignity and well-being of individuals, a view that challenges the realpolitik privilege given to the "national interest." The United States is directly associated with sponsoring many of these covenants and has ratified several others.

2. The Law of Armed Conflict. Somewhat protean and uneven, this represents the gradual emergence of a legal consensus on what is, and what is not, permissible during a state of war. It also comprises the various humanitarian agreements that determine the customary "law of war" and that attempt to reduce the oxymoronic element in this ancient debate.

3. International Criminal Law. This concerns any individual, including an agent of any state, who commits direct and grave atrocities against either his "own" citizens or those of another state; covered here are genocide, crimes against humanity, and other crimes of war. The Rome Statute, which also establishes an International Criminal Court for the trial of individuals, including governmental offenders, is the codified summa of this law as revised and updated since the Nuremberg precedent. It commands the signatures of most governments as well as, since 31 December 2000, that of the United States.

4. Domestic Law and the Law of Civil Remedies. Most governments have similar laws that govern crimes such as murder, kidnapping, and larceny, and many of them treat any offender from any country as the same. These laws in many cases permit a citizen of any country to seek redress in the courts of the offender's "host" country or country of citizenship. In United States law, one particularly relevant statute is the Alien Tort Claims Act.

The United States is the most generous in granting immunity to itself and partial immunity to its servants, and the most laggard in adhering to international treaties (ratifying the Genocide Convention only in 1988 and signing the Covenant on Civil and Political Rights only in 1992). And the provisions of the Rome Statute, which would expose Kissinger to dire punishment if they had been law from as early as 1968, are not retroactive. The

Nuremberg principles, however, were in that year announced by an international convention to have no statute of limitations. International customary law would allow any signatory country (again exempting the United States) to bring suit against Kissinger for crimes against humanity in Indochina.

More importantly, United States federal courts have been found able to exercise jurisdiction over crimes such as assassination, kidnapping, and terrorism, even when these are supposedly protected by the doctrine of state or sovereign immunity. Of a number of landmark cases, the most salient one is the finding of the DC Circuit Court in 1980, concerning the car-bomb murder, by Pinochet's agents, of Orlando Letelier and Ronni Moffitt. The court held that "[w]hatever policy options may exist for a foreign country," the Pinochet regime "has no 'discretion' to perpetrate conduct designed to result in the assassination of an individual or individuals, action that is clearly contrary to the precepts of humanity as recognized in both national and international law." Reciprocally speaking, this would apply to an American official seeking to assassinate a Chilean. Assassination was illegal both as a private and a public act when Henry Kissinger was in power and when the attacks on General Schneider of Chile and President Makarios of Cyprus took place.

As the Hinchey report to Congress in 2000 now demonstrates that US government agents were knowingly party to acts of torture, murder, and "disappearance" by Pinochet's death squads, Chilean citizens will be able to bring suit in America under the Alien Tort Claims Act, which grants US federal courts "subject-matter jurisdiction" over a claim when a non-US citizen sues for a civil wrong committed in violation of a US treaty or other international law. Chilean relatives of the "disappeared" and of General Schneider have recently expressed an interest in doing so, and l am advised by several international lawyers that Henry Kissinger would indeed be liable under such proceedings.

The Alien Tort Claims Act would also permit victims in other countries, such as Bangladesh or Cambodia, to seek damages from Kissinger, on the model of the recent lawsuit held in New York against Li Peng, among the

Chinese Communist officials most accountable for the 1989 massacre in Tiananmen Square.

A significant body of legal theory can be brought to bear on the application of "customary law" to the bombardment of civilians in Indochina. The Genocide Convention was not ratified by the United States until 1988. In 1951, however, it was declared by the International Court of Justice to be customary international law. The work of the International Law Commission is in full agreement with this view. There would be argument over whether the numberless victims were a "protected group" under existing law, and also as to whether their treatment was sufficiently indiscriminate, but such argument would place heavy burdens on the defense as well as the prosecution.*

An important recent development is the enforcement by third countries – notably Spain – of the international laws that bind all states. Baltasar Garzón, the Spanish judge who initiated the successful prosecution of General Pinochet, has also secured the detention in Mexico of the Argentine torturer Ricardo Miguel Cavallo, who is now held in prison awaiting extradition. The parliament of Belgium has recently empowered Belgian courts to exercise jurisdiction over war crimes and breaches of the Geneva Convention committed anywhere in the world by a citizen of any country. This practice, which is on the increase, has at minimum the effect of limiting the ability of certain people to travel or to avoid extradition. The Netherlands, Switzerland, Denmark, and Germany have all recently employed the Geneva Conventions to prosecute war criminals for actions committed against non-nationals by non-nationals. The British House of Lords decision in the matter of Pinochet has also decisively negated the defense of "sovereign immunity" for acts committed by a government or by those following a government's orders. This has led in turn to Pinochet's prosecution in his own country.

There remains the question of American law. Kissinger himself admits (see page 105) that he knowingly broke the law in continuing to supply

---

* See especially Nicole Barrett: "Holding Individual Leaders Responsible for Violations of Customary International Law," *Columbia Human Rights Law Review*, Spring 2001.

American weapons to Indonesia, which in turn used them to violate the neutrality of a neighboring territory and to perpetrate gross crimes against humanity. Kissinger also faces legal trouble over his part in the ethnic cleansing of the British colonial island of Diego Garcia in the early 1970s, when indigenous inhabitants were displaced to make room for a United States military base. Lawyers for the Chagos Islanders have already won a judgment in the British courts on this matter, which now moves to a hearing in the United States. The torts cited are "forced relocation, torture, and genocide."

In this altered climate, the United States faces an interesting dilemma. At any moment, one of its most famous citizens may be found liable for terrorist actions under the Alien Tort Claims Act, or may be subject to an international request for extradition, or may be arrested if he travels to a foreign country, or may be cited for crimes against humanity by a court in an allied nation. The non-adherence by the United States to certain treaties and its reluctance to extradite make it improbable that American authorities would cooperate with such actions, though this would gravely undermine the righteousness with which Washington addresses other nations on the subject of human rights. There is also the option of bringing Kissinger to justice in an American court with an American prosecutor. Again the contingency seems a fantastically remote one, but, again, the failure to do so would expose the country to a much more obvious charge of double standards than would have been apparent even two years ago.

The burden therefore rests with the American legal community and with the American human-rights lobbies and non-governmental organizations. They can either persist in averting their gaze from the egregious impunity enjoyed by a notorious war criminal and lawbreaker, or they can become seized by the exalted standards to which they continually hold everyone else. The current state of suspended animation, however, cannot last. If the courts and lawyers of this country will not do their duty, we shall watch as the victims and survivors of this man pursue justice and vindication in their own dignified and painstaking way, and at their own expense, and we shall be put to shame.

A FRAGRANT FRAGMENT

I AM TAKING the liberty of reproducing a correspondence, initially between Henry Kissinger and myself, which began in the *New York Times Book Review* in the fall of the year 2000. In a review (reprinted below) of *The Arrogance of Power*, the work by Anthony Summers and Robbyn Swan to which direct reference is made on page 13 of this book, I had essentially summarized and condensed the case against Nixon's and Kissinger's private and illicit diplomacy during the 1968 election; a case made much more fully in Chapter 1 here [see pages 8–15]. I also made reference to some other Nixon-era crimes and misdemeanors.

This drew a rather lengthy and – to put it no higher – distinctly bizarre reply from Kissinger. Its full text is also appended, together with the responses that it occasioned in its turn. (I have no means of knowing why Kissinger recruited former General Brent Scowcroft as his co-signer, unless it was for the reassurance of human company as well as the solidarity of a well-rewarded partner in the firm of Kissinger Associates.)

The correspondence makes three convenient points. It undermines pseudo-lofty attempts by Kissinger and his defenders to pretend that this book, or better say the arguments contained in it, are beneath their notice. They have already attempted to engage, in other words, and have withdrawn in disorder. Second, it shows the extraordinary mendacity, and reliance upon mendacity and upon non-credible but hysterical denial, that characterizes the Kissinger style. Third, it supplies another small window into the nauseating record of "rogue state" internal affairs.

Review by Christopher Hitchens
The Arrogance of Power: The Secret World of Richard Nixon.
Anthony Summers with Robbyn Swan.

In one respect at least, the memoirs of Henry Kissinger agree with *Sideshow*, William Shawcross's report on the bombing of Cambodia. Both books confirm that Richard Nixon rather liked people to fear his own madness. In the fall of 1969, for example, he told Kissinger to warn the Soviet ambassador that the President was "out of control" on Indochina, and capable of anything. Kissinger claims that he regarded the assignment as "too dangerous" to carry out. But, as Anthony Summers now instructs us:

> Three months earlier, however, Kissinger had sent that very same message by proxy when he instructed Len Garment, about to leave on a trip to Moscow, to give the Soviets "the impression that Nixon is somewhat 'crazy' – immensely intelligent, well organized and experienced to be sure, but at moments of stress or personal challenge unpredictable and capable of the bloodiest brutality." Garment carried out the mission, telling a senior Brezhnev advisor that Nixon was "a dramatically disjointed personality . . . more than a little paranoid . . . when necessary, a cold-hearted butcher." The irony, the former aide reflected ruefully in 1997, was that everything he had told the Russians turned out to be "more or less true."

The great merit of *The Arrogance of Power* is that it takes much of what we already knew, or thought we knew (or darkly suspected), and refines and confirms and extends it. The inescapable conclusion, well bodyguarded by meticulous research and footnotes, is that in the Nixon era the United States was, in essence, a "rogue state." It had a ruthless, paranoid and unstable leader who did not hesitate to break the laws of his own country in order to violate the neutrality, menace the territorial integrity or destabilize the internal affairs of other nations. At the close of this man's reign, in an episode more typical of a banana republic or a "people's democracy," his own secretary of defense, James Schlesinger, had to instruct the Joint Chiefs of Staff to disregard any military order originating in the White House.

Schlesinger had excellent grounds for circumspection. Not only had he learned that Nixon had asked the Joint Chiefs "whether in a crunch there was support to keep him in power," but he had also been told the following by Joseph Laitin, public affairs spokesman of the Office of Management and Budget. On his way to the West Wing in the spring of 1974, Laitin recalls:

> I'd reached the basement, near the Situation Room. And just as I was about to ascend the stairway, a guy came running down the stairs two steps at a time. He had a frantic look on his face, wild-eyed, like a madman. And he bowled me over, so I kind of lost my balance. And before I could pick myself up, six athletic-looking young men leapt over me, pursuing him. I suddenly realized that they were Secret Service agents, that I'd been knocked over by the president of the United States.

Summers, a former BBC correspondent who has written biographies of Marilyn Monroe and J. Edgar Hoover, makes us almost spoiled for choice as we seek an explanation for this delirious interlude and others like it. Nixon might have been intoxicated; it took very little alcohol to make him belligerent, and he became even more thuggish and incoherent when he threw in a few sleeping pills as well. He might have been hypermedicated, and he may have helped himself to a very volatile anticonvulsant called Dilantin, given to him by a campaign donor rather than prescribed by a physician. He might have been in a depressive or psychotic state; for three decades and in great secrecy he consulted a psychotherapist named Dr Arnold A. Hutschnecker. He may even have believed the Jews were after him; on numberless occasions he used his dirtiest mouth to curse at Jewish plots and individuals.

The most arresting chapter gives us conclusive reason to believe that Nixon and his associates – especially Attorney General John Mitchell and

Vice President Spiro Agnew – consciously sabotaged the Vietnam peace negotiations in Paris in the fall of 1968. Elements of this story have surfaced before, in books by – among others – Clark Clifford and Richard Holbrooke, Seymour Hersh and William Bundy. But this is the most convincing account to have appeared so far, relying as it does on wiretaps released to Summers by the Federal Bureau of Investigation. Many senior Democrats knew this ghastly secret but kept it to themselves, if only because L.B.J. had lawfully – if shamefacedly – bugged Nixon and his co-conspirators, as well as the South Vietnamese embassy. (The FBI intercept cables are reproduced here.)

Using a series of extremist and shady intermediaries, the Nixon campaign covertly assured the South Vietnamese generals that if they boycotted President Lyndon B. Johnson's dearly bought conference (which they ultimately did on the very eve of the election) they would get a more sympathetic administration. Irony is too feeble a word for what they actually got: a losing war, protracted for four years and concluded – with much additional humiliation – on the same terms that Johnson and Hubert Humphrey had been offering in 1968. Summers has spoken to all the surviving participants, including the dramatic go-between figure of Anna Chennault, who now regards even herself as one of those betrayed by this foul deal. Almost half the names on that wall in Washington are inscribed with a date after Nixon and Kissinger took office. We still cringe from counting the number of Vietnamese, Laotians and Cambodians. Nixon's illegal and surreptitious conduct not only prolonged an awful war but also corrupted and subverted a crucial presidential election: the combination must make it the most wicked action in American history.

Summers speculates that fear of disclosure might supply the motive for the Watergate burglary, an element in the tainting of yet a second election. Again, though, he spoils us for choice. If Nixon's mobsters were not looking for Democratic opposition research on the 1968 treason, they were looking for evidence that the Democrats either knew about bribes to the president from Howard Hughes or, much more probably, that they knew about secret subventions paid to Nixon and Agnew by the Greek military dictatorship. Nice choices, you will agree; it has taken some effort to narrow them down to those tasteful three (with a side bet on a prostitution racket that would have implicated both major parties).

For connoisseurs there is more detail – about the shenanigans of Nixon's crony, Bebe Rebozo, in the Bahamas; about underhand dealing with the Mafia in Cuba; and about the slow public martyrdom of Mrs Nixon, who, Summers says, may have been a victim of physical as well as mental cruelty. Too often for my taste, Summers employs the weasel word "reportedly," which ought to be banned. But he usually goes no farther than his evidence. And two serious and consistent themes assert themselves. Richard Nixon was able, time and again, to employ overseas entanglements to make end runs around American democracy. Short of money? The shah, or the Greek junta, or some friendly but inconvenienced multinational, will provide the dough, redeemable in arms trades or rakeoffs or an imaginative new line on human rights. Stuck for an issue? Embrace the very despots – Brezhnev or Mao – whose demonization has fueled your career thus far. Polls narrowing? Sell your own country by conducting off-the-record two-track diplomacy with tinpot clients, as in 1968.

The second theme involves an attraction to violence that perhaps only Hutschnecker's posthumous notes will explain. Like many law-and-order types, Nixon had a relish for rough stuff and police provocation. He seems to have helped encourage the mayhem that both disfigured and transfigured his tour of Latin America as vice president in 1958. As president, he can be heard on tape agreeing to the employment of Teamster bullies to batter antiwar demonstrators ("Yeah.... They've got guys who'll go in and knock their heads off"). This is the same duplicitous, gloating, insecure man who embellished his own mediocre war record in order to run for Congress, who adored obscene talk but was a poor hand with the fair sex, and who affected cloth-coat austerity while dabbling all his life in slush funds. A small man who claimed to be for the little guy, but was at the service of the fat cats. A pseudo-intellectual who hated and resented the real thing. Summers has completed the work of many predecessors, and made the task of his successors very difficult. In the process, he has done an enormous service by describing, to the citizens of a nation founded on law and right, the precise obscenity of that moment when the jutting jaw of a would-be Caesar collapses into the slobbering underlip of a weak and self-pitying king.

In Defense of Nixon

To the Editor:

We would like to raise some questions of fact about Christopher Hitchens's tendentious account of a tendentious book, Anthony Summers's "Arrogance of Power" (Oct. 8).

1. Neither of us was associated with Richard Nixon during the 1968 election campaign, but the allegations that he blocked a Johnson administration Vietnam peace initiative remain, in our view, allegations unsubstantiated by persuasive evidence. In any case, the record shows that the South Vietnamese foot-dragging (alleged to be at the behest of Nixon underlings) – even if the account were true – could not have had the consequences that Summers claims. The expanded Paris peace talks began in early November, and any delay was therefore very brief; Nixon – as president-elect and at the peak of his leverage – encouraged President Nguyen Van Thieu of South Vietnam to cooperate with the Johnson administration. Moreover, if the issue is political motivation, any discussion of this question has to begin with the indications from Soviet archives that Soviet leaders were led to believe that a main motive of rushing the bombing halt and peace talks was to get *Hubert Humphrey* elected.

2. It also needs to be borne in mind that the expanded Paris talks, once they began, were about procedure, not substance. Those talks immediately deadlocked, not on the substance of how to end the war but on whether the Vietcong guerrillas should have the same status at the table as the government of South Vietnam. No substantive proposal of any kind was put forward by the Johnson administration. It is therefore nonsense to assert

that Nixon in 1972 achieved no better terms than what Lyndon Johnson was "offering" in 1968. (Hanoi rejected compromise terms until 1972.)

3. The reviewer plays the usual numbers game with American soldiers killed in action, claiming that nearly half occurred on Nixon's watch. One-third would be more nearly accurate. But that is not the essence of the misrepresentation. When Nixon came into office, America had already suffered 36,000 soldiers killed in action. Of the 20,000 killed in the Nixon period, 12,000 occurred in the first year before any new policy could take effect, 9,000 in the first six months – clear legacies of the previous administration. When Nixon came in, American soldiers killed in action had run at an average rate of 1,500 per month for a year. At the end of his first term, they had been reduced to 50 per month. When Nixon entered office, American troops in Vietnam stood at 525,000 and were still increasing according to plans made in the Johnson administration. In 1972, they had been reduced to 25,000.

4. The Nixon administration concluded the first strategic arms control agreement and the first agreement banning biological weapons; opened relations with China; ended the decades-long crisis over Berlin; launched the Arab–Israeli peace process; and initiated the Helsinki negotiations, generally accepted as weakening the Soviets' control of their satellite empire and fostering German unification. Are these the actions of a "rogue" leader, as Hitchens calls Nixon?

5. Nixon was a strategist. He did want the notion to get around, as a strategic ploy, that if provoked by a foreign aggressor, he might respond disproportionately. But it is important here to separate the Nixon who sometimes expressed extreme statements to his confidants for dramatic or rhetorical effect and the Nixon who never made a really serious international move without the most careful and cautious analysis. It is laughable to imagine Richard Nixon ordering a domestic coup. Defense Secretary James Schlesinger did apparently in Nixon's last days direct the Joint Chiefs of Staff to ignore orders from their commander in chief – an unprecedented arrogation of authority. Whatever his motives, Schlesinger never came to either of us (or anyone else, so far as we know) with his concerns and what to do about them.

6. As for the story by Joe Laitin (a close associate of Schlesinger) that a frenetic Nixon came tearing down the stairs two at a time, pursued by six Secret Service agents, and literally knocked Laitin over – no way. Nixon could not have gone down a set of stairs two at a time if his life depended on it.

Henry A. Kissinger
New York
Brent Scowcroft
Washington
[*November 5 2000*]

Nixon Descending

To the Editor:

In reading Henry A. Kissinger and Brent Scowcroft's spirited defense of Richard Nixon (Letters, Nov. 5), I was surprised that they felt it necessary in making their case to say I had fabricated the details of my strange encounter with the president. I was there; they weren't.

However, they miss the point. Whether the president bowled me over or not is unimportant. I cannot swear that he was descending the stairs two at a time, three at a time or one at a time. All I can say is that the desperate look on his face as he was pursued by the Secret Service agents alarmed me and prompted my call to Defense Secretary James Schlesinger. Because I had direct access to Schlesinger, having worked with him for years, I was able to report the raw details of the incident immediately after it happened. As Kissinger and Scowcroft well know, history cannot be tampered with, and suggesting I lied about my encounter with President Nixon can't change what actually took place.

Joe Laitin
Bethesda, Md.
[*November 19 2000*]

Nixoniana

To the Editor:

In his and Brent Scowcroft's letter (Nov. 5), former Secretary of State Henry A. Kissinger denied having been associated with Defense Secretary James Schlesinger in directing the Joint Chiefs of Staff to ignore orders from President Richard Nixon. As one who during 1973–75 served on one of the Battle Staff units, on permanent standby to brief the president and top commanders in the event of a nuclear crisis, I know otherwise. As I have testified in secret debriefings and in both open and closed sessions of House and Senate committees as far back as 1975, Kissinger signed or countersigned at least three such orders in the final year of the Nixon presidency. I have so testified under penalty of perjury several times.

After the first such order in 1973 signed by Kissinger, the Joint Chiefs demanded that any subsequent ones be countersigned by at least one other Nixon cabinet officer. A second such order, again an instruction not to obey the president until further notice, was signed by Kissinger and, to the best of my recollection, Elliot Richardson. At least one other was jointly signed by Kissinger and Defense Secretary Schlesinger. Such orders were always sent "Top Secret, Eyes Only, Limited Distribution," bypassing other traffic. Sometimes they remained in effect for a week, most times only two to four days. The orders were issued at times of perceived Nixon mental instability, I repeatedly received them in my own hands, as did numerous others serving in sensitive nuclear control positions during that last horrific year of the Nixon presidency.

BARRY A. TOLL
Painesville, Ohio
[*December 12 2000*]

To the Editor:

The letter by Henry Kissinger and Brent Scowcroft, referring to our Nixon biography, "The Arrogance of Power," was an inept barrage. They assert that allegations of Nixonian sabotage of the 1968 Johnson peace effort are "unsubstantiated by persuasive evidence," then fail to counter any of our detailed analysis – which includes the recently released record of F.B.I. surveillance conducted on the eve of the election that brought Nixon to power.

Kissinger and Scowcroft cite Soviet archival sources, of all things, to insinuate that the Johnson peace initiative was just a political ploy "to get Hubert Humphrey elected." Any reading of the record of the pivotal White House meetings, available at the Johnson Library, dispels that notion. But even if that had been the case, it would not mitigate the offense indicated by the mass of information suggesting that Nixon did the unconscionable – as an unelected political candidate he meddled in the government's conduct of highly sensitive peace negotiations.

Readers of our book will find that we account, page by page, for our sources – which included more than a thousand interviews. Had Kissinger granted us an interview, we would have faithfully reported his views on relevant matters. We made nine written requests over a two-year period, but he ducked and weaved and never came through.

ANTHONY SUMMERS
ROBBYN SWAN
Cappoquin, Ireland
[*December 12 2000*]

Unpublished

To the Editor:

I suppose it is a distinction of some sort to be attacked at such length by Henry Kissinger and (for some reason) his business partner General Brent Scowcroft. It is certainly fascinating to see the evident nervousness with which they approach the allegations I made.

The record of Henry Kissinger's underhand involvement with the Nixon presidential campaign of 1968 is so extensively documented by now, including by Nixon himself, that one rubs the bleary eyes to read a denial of it. "Neither of us," write the two men, "was associated" with that campaign. Misery is said to love company; I have never bothered to inquire whether General Scowcroft played any part in that unhappy episode but his own modesty – perhaps disappointment – only serves to put his co-author's credibility in starker contrast with the facts. Mr Kissinger was hired as Nixon's principal advisor for national security as soon as the election was over, even though the two men had met only once. It was, moreover, Nixon's first appointment. Does Kissinger now deny that this was unconnected to the many surreptitious services performed by him, from Paris, for John Mitchell and for Nixon himself? If so, the flabbergasting denial of established facts would be interesting only insofar as it suggested something hitherto unguessed-at: the prickings of an uneasy conscience.

I make this perhaps unwarrantable suggestion because of a peculiar formulation later in the same paragraph, where Mr Kissinger (I've done with Scowcroft for now), says that:

> the record shows that the South Vietnamese foot-dragging (alleged to be at the behest of Nixon underlings) – *even if the account were true* – could not have had the consequence that Summers claims. The expanded Paris peace talks began in early November, and any delay was therefore very brief; Nixon – as president-elect and at the peak of his leverage – encouraged President Nguyen Van Thieu of South Vietnam to cooperate with the Johnson administration. (Italics added.)

This is a finely crafted paragraph and no mistake. But it is also very dishonestly argued. The South Vietnamese foot-dragging is not "alleged" but has been asserted and extensively documented. If the other emphasis of "alleged" is the intended one, then it was not at the "behest of underlings" – the now-familiar "deniable" scheme whereby the chief is never told what his deputies do – but at the direct instigation of Nixon himself. This has been solidly phrased by many Democratic and Republican high-level participants in these momentous events, and is not challenged, let alone rebutted, by Kissinger. "Early November" may sound suitably autumnal as a description of the seasonal setting of these same events, but it stretches to cover the date of the election itself and is thus designed to obscure what it purports to illuminate. What Kissinger means is that in the short interval when the actual "foot-dragging" took place, and as a thinkable consequence of that precise interval, one regime replaced another in the White House. That is, after all, the whole hypothesis (and the whole accusation) in the first place. Once President, Nixon did indeed appear to hew to the Johnson line – which is another element in the case against him and his newly promoted "National Security Advisor," who had no principled differences with that line to begin with.

The preceding and succeeding passages also betray unease. Kissinger does not say that there is no evidence for this grave allegation. He says that the evidence is not persuasive. Does he care to say what is unpersuasive about the evidence adduced by so many historians and participants, from the hawkish Bundy and Haldeman to the more skeptical Clark Clifford? Evidently he does not. Instead, there comes a breathtaking and highly suggestive change of subject:

> If the issue is political motivation, any discussion of this question has to begin with the indications from Soviet archives that Soviet leaders were led to believe that a main motive of rushing the bombing halt and peace talks was to get *Hubert Humphrey* elected. (Italics in original.)

This clumsily constructed sentence deserves a close parsing. Apparently, political motivation is an allowable sub-text of the argument over the Paris negotiations after all, since if it can be alleged – actually only suggested – about the Democratic incumbents it can also surely be alleged about their Republican opponents. So one is grateful for Kissinger's perhaps inadvertent concession of common ground. However, if the Johnson–Humphrey regime sought to time the talks for their own electoral purposes (and this writer was not and is not in any position to approve of anything they undertook) then they did so in public view, and as the legally elected and constituted government of the United States. In that capacity, too, they would have been subject to the judgment of the voters as to their likely opportunism. Whereas Messrs Nixon, Agnew, Mitchell and Kissinger (only one of them so far unindicted for one abuse of power or another) would have been conducting a "diplomacy" with unaccredited interlocutors, illegal under the Logan Act, concealed not only from both the public and denominated negotiators of the country but also from its electorate! This indeed is part of the essential *gravamen* of the charge. To put the two notions on the same footing, and to lard them with vague and unsupported innuendoes about "Soviet" knowledge, is to take the same attitude to the United States Constitution that Kissinger was later to adopt towards the Chilean one.

It is obviously true to say, in a military-technocratic sense, that there is some extensive cross-over between the war as waged by Johnson and Humphrey and the war as "inherited" by Nixon and Kissinger. To that extent, some of the assertions of point (3) need not be disputed. ("Onethird would be more nearly accurate." Good grief – so Kissinger has been counting them after all, while daring to accuse me of playing "the usual numbers game.") However, if the "legacy" transmitted from one administration to the next was indeed passed through a filter of illegal secret dealing with an undisclosed third power – as has been authoritatively argued, and as the outgoing administration certainly believed – and if the effect of this was to enhance the level of violence rather than to diminish it, then the case for regarding Mr Kissinger as a war criminal, careless only of *American* deaths, is complete on those terms alone.

Your readers might care to note that in seeking further to dilute the above implications, he says nothing to my original point about hugely increased Vietnamese, Cambodian and Laotian casualties during the years 1969–1975; a period when the war and its devastation was extended into large new tracts of formerly neutral and civilian territory. Such an omission cannot be accidental; it is the sort of "oversight" which results from a racist world-view and hopes – I am sure in vain – to concentrate the attention and sympathy of your audience only upon its "own" losses.

The remaining paragraphs of his letter are replete with boilerplate propaganda and pitiful falsehood, much of it ably disposed of by the later letters you have printed from Mr Laitin and Mr Toll. My forthcoming book *The Trial of Henry Kissinger* will, I hope, supply the refutation of the residual claims.

CHRISTOPHER HITCHENS
Washington, DC

[A PS for readers: I do not complain of not seeing my own letter in print; it was excessively lengthy and I had already had my say in the columns of the *Book Review*. I also delayed too long in sending it, in case Kissinger – or even the hapless Scowcroft – might choose to take on the annihilating replies they had received from Laitin and Toll. But answer came there none, so I allowed myself the satisfaction of finishing an argument Kissinger had started and then abandoned.]

APPENDIX II

THE DEMETRACOPOULOS LETTER

DOBROVIR & GEBHARDT

SUITE 1105

1025 VERMONT AVENUE, N. W.

WASHINGTON, D. C. 20005

(202) 347-8118

TELEX: 6503136357

WILLIAM A. DOBROVIR
JOSEPH D. GEBHARDT
ROBERT L. BAUM
ROBIN A. FRADKIN
NINA JOAN KIMBALL

COUNSEL BETH L. DON

OF COUNSEL
ELIZABETH L. NEWMAN, P.C.

September 3, 1987

<u>BY MESSENGER</u>

Dr. Henry A. Kissinger
c/o James E. Wesner, Esq.
Ginsberg, Feldman, Weil & Bress
Suite 700
1250 Connecticut Avenue, N.W.
Washington, D.C. 20036

Dear Dr. Kissinger:

You will recall correspondence I sent to you, care of your attorney James Wesner, in 1980, concerning NSC documents referring to Elias P. Demetracopoulos. You never replied to those letters, in particular to the last, October 24, 1980, letter. From what you had told us through your attorney at that time, we were led to believe that neither you nor NSC possessed any of the described documents. Events since then require us to renew this matter with you.

1. Papers of Richard M. Nixon, released in May 1987, included John Dean files relating to Mr. Demetracopoulos, but no NSC files, as far as we know.

2. As you know (since we sent you copies), NSC released to us copies of computer indices showing that while you were National Security Advisor and Chairman of the "40 Committee," the NSC did have copies of documents relating to Mr. Demetracopoulos. NSC informed us that the documents, if not in the Nixon papers (as they do not seem to be), were taken by you and presumably repose in your personal files, those files sent to the National Archives, or those files you have deposited in the Library of Congress but which are closed to the public until 2001.

Dr. Henry A. Kissinger
September 3, 1987
Page 2

3. One of the NSC computer indices shows a document, dated December 18, 1970, which refers to "Mr. Demetracopoulos death in Athens prison." That was about the time that the first attempts were made by the Greek dictatorship to kidnap Mr. Demetracopoulos, then living in this country, presumably to spirit him back to Greece to his "death in [an] Athens prison." This has recently been documented in sworn statements of knowledgeable Greek officials. The Senate Select Committee on Intelligence, chaired by the late Sen. Frank Church, began investigating the incident in connection with its study of intelligence activities relating to Greece: but, according to Committee sources, as reported by Seymour Hersh in his book <u>The Price of Power</u>, you urged the Committee to drop the investigation, and it did so.

4. Documents released by the CIA since 1980 refer to briefings for then President Ford in October 1974. The document refers to a "trace paper" about Mr. Demetracopoulos, a "derogatory blind memo" and "the long Kissinger memo on Elias [Demetracopoulos]," "left ... with General Skowcroft." Copies of pertinent documents are enclosed.

You should be aware that after a great deal of discussion, correspondence and congressional investigation, both the FBI and then Director William Webster and the CIA under the late Director William Casey, acknowledged that their years of investigation turned up not a shred of "derogatory" information about Mr. Demetracopoulos. A copy of a document is enclosed.

We cannot help but assume that you possess <u>at least</u> a copy of "the long Kissinger memo" on Mr. Demetracopoulos, and you may also possess copies of the "trace paper" and the "derogatory blind memo."

Dr. Henry A. Kissinger
September 3, 1987
Page 3

We ask that, in order to complete the historical record you provide Mr. Demetracopoulos promptly with copies of the mentioned documents.

Sincerely yours,

William A. Dobrovir

Enclosures

jk

ACKNOWLEDGEMENTS

When *Harper's* magazine was good enough to publish the two long essays that together became the core of this book, my friend and publisher Rick MacArthur sent an early copy round to ABC News in New York. Since we had criticized the deference of the American media quite as much as we had attacked the moral sloth of the overfed American "human rights" community, he thought it was only fair to give *Nightline*'s producer the right of reply. After an interval, we got our answer. "Is there," said the top man at that top-rated Kissinger-showcasing show, "anything new here?"

Rick and I hugged ourselves with promised laughter at that. In Washington and New York and Los Angeles and every other cultural capital, the shallow demand for novelty is also an ally of a favorite spin-tactic of the powerful, which is to confront a serious allegation not by refusing to deny it but instead by trying to reclassify it as "old news." And of course, the joke was therefore on the producer, who had come up with a stale and predictable and exhausted response. (We later asked him if there was anything fresh about his question.)

Had it been asked in good faith, of course, that same question would still require a straight answer. Here it is. The information in this book is not "new" to the people of East Timor and Cyprus and Bangladesh and Laos and Cambodia, whose societies were laid waste by a depraved statecraft. Nor is it "new" to the relatives of the tortured and disappeared and murdered in Chile. But it *would* be new to anyone who relied on ABC News for information. It is not new to the degraded statesmen who agree to appear on that network in return for being asked flattering questions. But some of it might come as news to the many decent Americans who saw their own laws and protections violated, and their own money spent in their name but without their leave, for atrocious purposes that could not be disclosed, by the Nixon–Kissinger gang. Oh yes, this is an old story all right. But I hope and intend to contribute to writing its ending.

As a matter of fact, there *are* a few disclosures in the book; some of the new material shocked even its author. But I'm not here to acknowledge my own work. Wherever possible, I give credit and attribution in the narrative itself. Some debts must still be mentioned.

Nobody in Washington who takes on the Kissinger matter can ever be clear of debt to Seymour Hersh, who first contrasted the man's reputation with his actions, and by this method alone, as well as by heroic excavations of the record, began the slow process which will one day catch up with the worthless, evasive cleverness of official evil. This is a battle for transparency and for historical truth, among other things, and if Hersh has any rival in that area it is Scott Armstrong, founder of the National Security Archive, which has been deputizing as Washington's equivalent of a Truth and Justice Commission until the real thing comes along. ("Then let us pray that come it may . . .")

During their long absence from the moral radar-screen of the West, the people of East Timor could have had no better and braver friends than Amy Goodman and Allan Nairn. The family of Orlando Letelier, and the families of so many other Chilean victims, could always count on Peter Kornbluh, Saul Landau and John Dinges, who in Washington have helped keep alive a case of crucial importance that will one day be vindicated. Martin Edwin Anderson, Lucy Komisar, Mark Hertsgaard, Fred Branfman, Kevin Buckley, Lawrence Lifschultz will, I know, all recognize

themselves in my borrowings from their more original and more courageous work.

Sometimes a chat with an editor can be encouraging; sometimes not. I
was in the middle part of my first explanatory sentence with Lewis
Lapham, editor of *Harper's* magazine, when he broke in to say: "Done.
Write it. High time. We'll do it." I didn't trust myself then to thank him, as
I do now. So instead I got on with it, which I could not have done without
the unusual Ben Metcalf at the *Harper's* office. Together with Sarah Vos and
Jennifer Szalai, punctilious fact-checkers, we went over it again and again,
marvelously nauseated at the renewed realization that it was all true.

The current state of international human rights legislation is highly
inchoate. But, in an uneven yet seemingly discernible fashion, it is evolving
to the point where people like Kissinger are no longer above the law.
Welcome and unexpected developments have had a vertiginous effect: I
hope that my closing section on this area is out of date by the time it is published. For their help in guiding me through the existing statutes and
precedents, I am enormously obliged to Nicole Barrett of Columbia
University, to Jamin Raskin and Michael Tigar at the Washington College
of Law at American University, and to Geoffrey Robertson QC.

Patrick Lannan and the Lannan Foundation were both enthusiastic and
generous about this project, and kindly provided the seed-money that will
make its main conclusions available in television-documentary form.

There are very few mirthful moments in these pages. Still, I remember
so well the day in 1976 when Martin Amis, then my colleague at the *New
Statesman,* told me that his literary pages would serialize Joseph Heller's
Good as Gold. He showed me the proposed extract. Chapters 7 and 8 of that
novel, in particular, are imperishable satire, and must be read and reread.
(The relevant passage of sustained and obscene and well-reasoned abuse,
which shames the publishing industry as well as the journalistic racket for
its complicity with this deceitful and humorless toad, begins with the sentence: "Even that fat little fuck Henry Kissinger was writing a book!") I later
became a friend of Joe Heller, whose death in 1999 was a calamity for so

many of us, and my last acknowledgement is to the invigorating effect of his warm, broad-minded, hilarious, serious, and unquenchable indignation.

Christopher Hitchens
Washington, DC, 25 January 2001

INDEX